IN SEARCH OF A ONE-WOMAN'S-MAN

(....a must-read for every single woman seeking holy matrimony.....)

Author: Winnie Gichohi Riley

Copyright © 2010 by Winnie Gichohi Riley

In Search Of A One-Woman's-Man
(....a must-read for every single woman seeking holy
matrimony.....)
by Winnie Gichohi Riley

Printed in the United States of America

ISBN 9781615799046

Unless otherwise indicated, Bible quotations are taken from The KJV Rainbow Study Bible. Copyright © 1986 by Rainbow Studies International.

www.xulonpress.com

Book Dedication

I dedicate this book first of all to The Lord who created me, and secondly to my husband, to whom the title refers - my One-Woman's-Man. I am particularly overjoyed that the Lord gave me a husband who is a dedicated servant of the body of Christ, giving us not only a matrimonial bond but also a partnership as servants in the Kingdom of God.

OUR MISSION STATEMENT:

We are sensitive to the voice of God as touching on our lives and on the lives of others. We have kept a close walk with God due to constant supplication, fervent prayer and fasting.

We are vessels being used of God and will continue accepting to be used of him.

We are friends of God:

Richard and Winnie Gichohi Riley

Special thanks goes out to all our prayer partners, _with special mention to our head Intercessor and spiritual mom: Sis Beatrice Boyd of California, USA._ God bless you all!!!

Table of contents

CHAPTER 1

a) <u>Definition of a One-Woman's-Man:</u>

One of the largest causes of divorce is infidelity. When a married man starts seeing another woman, he brings all sorts of excuses justifying this act. But the bottom line of infidelity is that it is in the character of an individual man, something deep in his genetic make up, something that can **never change**.

This is why you see a nice woman, being so nice to her man in fact, extra nice. Giving him first class treatment. But the man still wanders. You see, this beats common sense. Some will give justification and this leaves a woman feeling inferior and inadequate. Some men will even leave a very brilliant and good woman for another who is just the opposite. But let no-one lie to you: infidelity is something in-born (in men as well as in women). It is largely hereditary. Let me give my personal example:

I come from a family of a OWM. My father is indeed a faithful, loving, sober husband, and a tough father who has high standards of discipline for his children. Oh yes! my dad is the kind of dad no child would dare mess with. Sometimes I used to ask my mother about my dad's character as a husband especially after I grew up. And this is what she told me: "Winnie, there are men who will not be promiscuous - at all. It is in their character. But there is one thing you have to know - they comprise of a very tiny fraction of men. And this is because the largest percentage of men are by nature, unfaithful to their wives. Your father is a "One-Woman's-Man". When I reflected on this - especially being African by birth I had to believe her word because polygamy, and other forms of promiscuity are extremely widespread in Africa.

It was always my prayer to meet that OWM one day in my life. I have not accomplished it by my own strength and the road has been extremely rough, I must admit. The largest driving force has been my biological family and my church family. All the glory however goes to God because without him, I would not even have lead a life worth writing a book such as this. The Lord has humbled me and in him I glory. When I think of this book and those it will touch, it leads me to share the scripture:

Galatians 6:14 "But God forbid that I should glory, save in the cross of our Lord Jesus Christ,

by whom the world is crucified unto me, and I unto the world"

b) <u>Be a sincere Christian</u>

Creating for yourself a strong Christian foundation is the only way to build up a sustainable marriage.

Over and above being a woman, you are first and foremost called to be a Christian. A sincere Christian and not a seasonal one. Remember that you want not only to prosper here on earth, but to make sure you do not miss out in eternal life:

Philippians 3:14 "I Press towards the mark for the prize of the high calling of God in Jesus Christ".

The upright Christian marriage is not a place for a woman who is mediocre in her spiritual standards. Seek God first. Walk the walk of faith because Christianity is not a one-time deal with God, it is an every-day walk with him:

Matthew 6:33 "But seek ye first the kingdom of God and His righteousness and all these things shall be added unto you"

Woman! get your spiritual life in order!"'. And do you know why? If you do not set for yourself sincere Christian standards, you will also meet a man who is mediocre in his spirituality like the kind who go to church to look for wives, yet in reality, they are worldly men of the flesh. They will hoodwink you to believing that they are legitimate Christians, only to later discover that they are just in church to get you, and a short while into the marriage, they will go back to the world while you remain the woman in the house taking care of the children while the man continues with his promiscuity.

As a Christian woman the OWM you are looking for is that God fearing man who will love you according to God's standards. He will be the love of your life and you will both have a profound love for Jesus Christ who will be the center of your lives. Christian courtship and dating is first and foremost platonic: you have to totally do away with fornication and adultery. In **Exodus 20 v 14: "Thou shall not commit adultery**." Which is commandment no: 7. Why God commands us to keep away from sex before marriage is because he wants us to be spiritual; more so than any other time. Also we recall this great story in **Genesis 34** of how Shechem son of Hamor the Hivite raped Dinah daughter of Jacob and Leah. This act ultimately brought a pulverizing curse among the Hivites who were already a cursed nation even long before this act. Sexual sin is what begun the process of a curse among the Hivites. They were slain, their wives taken and property plundered. Pre-marital sex is always sinful in the eyes of God and those who Indulging in it create a destructive stronghold in their lives. Pre-marital sex is of the flesh as opposed to the spirit, and as you know, the flesh can never please God. For more details on this scripture, have a look at **Genesis 34.**

The bible speaks a lot on fornication. Here is another example, this time in the new Testament. **Colossians 3:5 "Mortify therefore your members which are upon the earth; fornication, unclean- liness, inordinate affection, evil concupiscence and covtousness which is idolatry".** Evil concu- piscence simply means 'evil desires'.

Do not get me wrong. The world too has the secular OWM - in fact many. I would advice you, as a Christian woman, to aspire for the God-fearing born-again OWM. Those who have secured OWM and are secular couples - oh! let them just thank their luck. Do not emulate them. When people choose to live a secular life, there is a big reason as to why they are locking God out of their lives and sooner or later they will pay, dearly.

There is also a category of secular OWM who are one-woman-man simply because they have no urge for other women. Some of them are possessive over their wives and practically cut off all her freedoms. This category of secular OWM simmer their wives to their graves. There are some who are also abusive: emotionally and physically. Concerning these categories of OWM I would dissuade you from emulating them or even aspiring to be married to one of them. Some women remark when they are in secular dating "Oh, he is nice"; "he loves me"; "we do not want to lead that boring Christian life"; "We want to be able to enjoy life". Please ladies on a point of advice, do not listen to any of that talk! As a Christian couple, we can assure you there is no happier life. As a woman married to a OWM, I can confess that I have never had such a full, satisfying and enjoyable life as I do now. Try God's way of searching for a husband I assure you that you will never regret it.

Some men try very hard to follow the things of God, but they have that nature in them, the nature of promiscuity. In the bible, we see them! David, Solomon...the list is endless. There were also OWM in the bible: Zachariah (the father of John the Baptist), Joseph (the father of Jesus) But when you are trusting God for a husband, you are

23

looking for the OWM. It does not mean that every Christian man (Or so they call themselves) qualifies as a OWM. When we look at men of the bible like David and Solomon, promiscuous men enjoy referencing them saying: 'hey! David had many women and so had Solomon'. Yes it is true that these men are great, real Biblical heroes. But God has not put them in the bible so that men can emulate their promiscuity and use it as a justification for infidelity. What we are to emulate from these men is their positive characteristics. We should abandon their negative qualities. And to remind you that these qualities were negative, recall how much God punished them for their promiscuity. Each time the bible talks of a sinful character, it continues to show what form of reproof they go through and what God does to restore them. Some people even say that if Jesus used to hang around sinners, they too have the right to do so. For sure, we see Jesus hanging out with a sinner like Zacchaeus. But at the end of visiting with Zacchaeus, Jesus converted Zacchaeus, averted him from his sinful ways and became a follower of Jesus. The woman at the well also after recognizing her sin ended up being a follower of Jesus. The same with Mary Magdalene who turned away from her life of prostitution. The woman caught in adultery, at the verge of almost being stoned to death, Jesus convinced the crowd not to stone her. But did Jesus tell her that it was ok to continue in adultery? No! he told her "Go and sin no more"...."

John 8 v 3 - 7; 10: "And the scribes and the Pharisees brought unto him a woman taken in adultery; and when they had set her in the midst, They say unto him, Master, this woman was taken in, in the very act. Now, Moses in the law com-

manded us, that such should be stoned; but what sayest thou? This they said, tempting him, that they might have to accuse him. But Jesus stooped down, and with his finger wrote on the ground, as though he heard them not. So they continued asking him, he lifted up himself, and said unto them, <u>he that is without sin among you, let him first cast a stone at her</u> ....v 10: ...When Jesus had lifted up himself and saw none but the woman, he said to her <u>woman, where are those thine accusers? hath no man condemned thee?</u> She said No man, Lord. And Jesus said unto her, <u>Neither do I condemn thee: GO AND SIN NO MORE!!!!!!"</u>

So God had a way of correcting these sins and did not advice the sinners to dwell in those sins. So as Christians when we identify with the sin we should also identify with God's word of correction. If we remember right, There is only one man in the bible that we are to emulate. And that was Jesus Christ. When we read the Bible, time and time again we are told to be Christ-like. We are to identify with God and God alone, because we are created in his image:

Leviticus 11 v 44: "For I am the Lord your God: ye shall therefore sanctify yourselves, and ye shall be holy; for I am holy."

Christ triumphed in this battle because he was not alone. We should take the same lane. So do not justify sin by saying that Jesus identified with sinners. The bible only shows us sinful men and women and then illustrates how they turned away from their sins. And those who adamantly remained sinful

27

where pulverized, usually to death. Whereas we are commanded to be Christ-like, let us remember that this does not give us a ticket to bliss. We are to fully follow Christ aware of the fact that we will be persecuted. But let us also remember that they crucified him!! We are further on told that he triumphed because in this battle he was not alone. We should take the same lane. I kindly beg you to Ignore those who tell you that you can put God on the exterior of your marriage and be happy: that's a lie.

c) <u>Christian dating: Platonic courtship.......</u>

There are two basic reasons why a man approaches a woman. It is either for marriage or for sex. Some men also have a platonic agenda but that is very rare. There are also reasons based upon professional affiliations. Some of these categories do not draw definite boundaries.

As a Christian woman, be very careful. If you had a sexually active life before salvation, be careful not to fellowship with the devil once again. There are Christian men who are so disillusioned by the promiscuity in women that they will ask you for sex even when you are a Christian. They have an agenda to filter their choices by using the elimination method. Immediately you consent to sex, or show indication of consent, Down! they drop you. Others will not even go all the way to having sex with you. But women who have been in the flesh know how to seduce men. Once a serious Christian man searching for a wife discovers that you are willing to lure him into sex, he damps you and continues on his quest for the real God fearing woman who is pure in mind, body and spirit. The reason why they do so is because your actions indicate a habitual trait. So ladies, keep to the rules and you will not go wrong. There should be no sex before marriage....absolutely no sex before marriage. Wait patiently for your wedding night.

The most crucial reason why courting couples should not have a sexual agenda is a litmus test meant to define sexual behavior. Are you sexually adventurous? There will be periods of time in a marriage when a married woman will not be totally efficient in her sexual performance for example during and after pregnancy. If you have always had sex with your boyfriend (I'm talking to women of the world), how will you tell of the extent to which he can go without sex? Yes, he will marry you. But you will be in for a big surprise when you become pregnant or sick. So in essence why God commands us to keep off unwedded sex and especially during dating and courtship - is because you need to study the sexual habits of this man you are dating.

Let's look at the worldly men. In general, men who approach a woman for sexual relationship that is not sealed in marriage have an agenda at the back of their minds: So that they can quit when it suits them because the driving force of the relationship is selfish lust and not genuine love. They are looking out for cheap sex. You simply cannot merge secular standards and Christian standards and expect to yield a happy marriage. And for those men who are not born-again but are faithful to their wives, you wives, just count yourself very fortunate that you got married to a OWM. And please be warned that this pattern is the exception and not the rule. The fact that you missed to link up with that promiscuous man in spite of having a secular courtship does not mean that you can go advising young women to follow your example. You will just be

31

digging a hole for them to fall into. You are a bad influence to the Christian society.

This is where we distinguish worldly standards from Christian standards. The world has nondescript sayings like "love without sex is like tea without sugar"; or some secular psychologists say that the relationship between a man and woman is only 3o% without sex. Some get even more derisive of Christian standards by saying that being in a platonic relationship is like eating candy with the wrapper on.............and the list goes on and on. Let us remember that our duty is to God and not to the world. The day you find yourself with a promiscuous husband because of not heeding the word of the Lord, or the day you find yourself with HIV infection, or an unwanted pregnancy these people ridiculing your moral standards will not help you. They will remain hands off while you suffer the consequences alone. If you go it alone without the counsel of God, willing to have him out of your affairs, remember that we serve a Lord who has good manners. He does not go to where he is uninvited. So You will be alone in your problems as a consequence of secular acts - and a melée it will be. Of course you will hit rock bottom and then recall that there was a God. But remember that God is kind and forgiving. But you have already complicated your own life by choosing your own way and as you know, you cannot unscramble a scrambled egg. Why ladies find themselves in this situation is because they choose to ignore God's counsel at the beginning. Taking God's counsel is God's own way of helping us make a foundation for our matrimonial life. The steps towards this are tough and you have to work towards it consistently and you can only do so by being a sincere Christian.

Let's take the example of the Christian woman who decides that it is too difficult to follow God's counsel when looking for a marriage partner. She takes secular steps in dating and courtship and eventual marriage. Then she tries to work out the marriage, but because God was not in it, the marriage turns out to be unhappy and its very existence is threatened. The most likely thing is that this woman will fall back to her God and that is good because God is a forgiving God and he's a God of a second chance. But then there are children, sexually transmitted diseases, a marriage contract, property.....the list is endless of things that are at stake. So for the sake of redeeming her marriage and all the consequences of this marriage, this woman goes back to her God.

The one thing I would like to urge all young Christian women: keep your eyes on God in spite of the circumstances in your dating. Have nothing, absolutely nothing to do with the flesh. No matter how long it takes because as you can see, if you mess it up, you will have to still go back to God and begin a relationship with God right from Square one. God requires that we cultivate a father-daughter relationship with him where we can speak to him daily in prayer, and listen to him daily through his daily word. Treat God with respect because the more you keep to his word, the less difficult your marriage will be. It does not mean that the marriage will be smooth. It just means you will soar above those problems because you went into the marriage with God's full blessings. Take God as a friend, have an amicable relationship with him. Do not treat him like a lawyer whom you run to when you are in a mess; or fire insurance to avoid losing your property in the fire! take him as a friend, and guess what? he will reciprocate!

Why a secular relationship is unhealthy for a woman, is that the largest proportion of these women work over-time to make the relationship last......unfortunately down the line, if a man is not willing to commit, he will not commit just because he has been having a sexual relationship with you. And more likely than not, he will damp you at the end of a very excruciating love affair. Women go into these relationships with all their hearts. When the men walk out, the women are left hurting for a long time after having wasted their time, resources, and she will be run down, and she will be emotionally drained, with a question on her mind. The wise woman in this category thinks twice and considers what it takes to keep a man. Let's for a moment look at a scenario where women from this type of a relationship pressurizes a man for marriage or the relationship brings fourth a child or children. This relationship will always be shaky because like the foolish man, this relationship has a foundation of sand - unlike the woman who has a relationship with the foundation of rock and that is Jesus Christ.

Early divorces, outrageous divorces, wife-abuse, accelerated unfaithfulness:

This happens in most marriages because as a woman, you have manipulated a man into marrying you and this does not mean that there a future in this kind of a marriage. Many of these men will get tired and move on to another woman especially when the woman gets older and begins giving birth. The older man will go ahead and get the younger women a 'trophy wife'.

This is simply the fact that relationships based on the flesh are not God-ordained. They are based on lust and temporary pleasure. After being a girl-friend or mistress of many years, it is like the man is finally saying "Bye! and extends a handshake - it was a pleasure knowing you, I would like us to give each other a break." Sex alone cannot sustain a relationship - marriage or other. Please check this with successfully married couples: sex accounts for just a minimal percentage of duties needed to uphold a marriage. It also goes a long way to prove that a marriage based on the wrong foundation may not go very far. A large number of women will try their best to salvage this, but most of those marriages are bound to disintegrate and when they do not they survive on a cliff's edge. The only foundation is Jesus Christ and there is none other:

Psalm 11v 3: "If the foundations be destroyed, what can the righteous do?"

The largest proportion of these marriages are totally pulverized by the enemy and it is now up to the woman to pick up her broken pieces, follow God's Ordinance and lay a foundation for a God-based marriage. It is never too late to start with God again. He is merciful and is a rewarder of those who diligently seek him. He is the master builder.

d) How my aunt soothed me through my first heart-break:

When I was in my mid-twenties, I once confided a heartbreak I was going through because my eldest paternal auntie Mrs. Rose Njimu (a successfully married mother of 5) gave me a great deal of counsel and I will always live to thank God for her. I met my high-school sweet-heart when I was 17. I will call him Bill for identity purposes, though this is not his name. It was typical first love. Just thinking of him used to consume me. He was a very handsome young man and I knew that I would have loved to spend the rest of my life with him. By then I was not born-again but I was a very well brought up Christian and my mother's counsel went with me wherever I went. So I knew that pre-marital sex was forbidden territory. Even morally, I knew that I was not ready for sex. So our love just consisted of writing love letters to each other. In senior high school, what we called "A" levels in Kenya, I was in a girls' boarding school in Eldoret, and he was in a boys' boarding school in Nairobi.. So we used to look out for each other's letters each week. On school holidays we could meet once or twice, he usually treated me to Dinner and we could go to the park and just talk and talk, usually about our future plans. One very major area of common interest was that we both studied French and we were aspiring to continue with it to University. We spoke about our future, career, family etc. We kept totally off sex, it was just a very warm love. He led me to believe that we would make a future together especially after University. So I was always exited by this thought. When we completed high school, we both qualified for University, and to study degrees that incorporated the French language. But we were admitted to different Universities about 22miles apart. When he joined Nairobi University, he became a born-again Christian. That was in 1988. I was still a church going Christian, though not born-again. He started avoiding me. He never once asked me to consider salvation. He could not even accept to attend church with me. By 1990, I was the one who kept the relationship alive by visiting him at his college hostel, usually unwelcome. By this time I was hurting badly. And then a few months down the line, my close friends at Nairobi University started enlightening me of his movements: a certain born-again lady at his class was often seen in his company. Those who were very close to me gave me inside information that pointed towards a sexual relationship. By this time I got really depressed. I was only 21 then and I was so disillusioned with the born-again campus group. They were fornicating! some of my classmates who knew about our relationship since high school were deriding me: "Winnie, you refused to give him your goods! that's why he took off". By the time we graduated, they were openly fornicating, it was no longer a secret. They were fornicating and still serving in the church youth group as "exemplary youths". It was shortly after graduating that I left for France for further studies, a disillusioned young woman about the life of men and what true Christianity meant. They later got married, but I wondered what Christianity had to offer. This is where born-again Christians miss the mark. They fail to be the right mirror for society. They cause so many people to fall especially when they try to emulate the Christian life-style. People of the world are comfortably saying: if born-again Christians can do it, why can't we?

The bible is condemning anyone who causes another to stumble or fall: **Romans 14 v 21: "It is good neither to eat flesh, nor drink wine, nor do any thing whereby thy brother stumbleth, or is offended or is made weak"** God's judgment will be upon you. So I narrated this story to Auntie Rose and this is what she told me, and I would like to advice any young woman who aspires to serve God with auntie Roses words. Her words were: "Winnie, how old are you now? are you not in your 20s?" and I affirmed. "I would like to inquire of you: if you were to be married even at the age of 30, and you have a life-span of up to 70 years, which years would be longer? years as a married woman or years as a single woman?" and I replied "years as a married woman" (In my family we have a very strong covenant of marriage and marriages are very stable - divorce is very minimal). "Then if you foresee that marriage will take up most of the years of your life, you better make the right choice". She looked me in the eye and told me "In fact, that man did you a great favor. Let him go, he has no principles. He would have messed up your life - away with trouble". You better wait and marry late, than marry in a hurry and mess your life. She herself married rather late in life-according to the marriageable age at that time, and she has a very stable marriage, a wonderful husband and five grown children who are very prosperous especially in the field of academics.

The next difficult option for any God fearing upright woman is to see for herself that she needs to link up with a man who truly fears God in order to find fulfillment in marriage. And truly speaking, those women who default on this even after such bitter experiences live lives of misery till their dying day. It does not matter that you brought fourth a child in an Un-Godly relationship. Once you repent and turn to God fully, you will not look behind. God can favor you with that God-fearing husband who will marry you regardless of having a child out of wedlock. So women! do not disqualify yourself from cleaning up your spiritual mess and seeking Christ afresh. God is in the business of rewarding, renewing and replenishing.

Here is scripture to encourage those women who had fallen into sexual sin before they dedicated their lives to Christ. Just repent, be humble and you will see what God can do for you:

Psalms 25: v 4-9 "Shew me thy ways, O Lord; teach me thy paths. Lead me in thy truth, and teach me: for thou art the God of my salvation; on thee do I wait all day. Remember, O Lord thy tender mercies and thy lovingkindness; for thy have been ever of old. Remember not the sins of my youth, nor my transgressions: according to thy mercy remember thou me for thy goodness' sake, O Lord. Good and upright is the Lord: therefore will he teach sinners in the way. The meek will he guide in judgment: and the meek will he teach his way"

The largest proportion of OWM consists of that group of men who fear and serve God. And as I mentioned earlier, these men comprise of a very strict minority. You see the devil will also have his counterfeits, and you will see men purporting to be Christians in churches even in some churches - occupying positions of leadership. And when you examine them, you realize that they do not lead a bible life. Beware of these because they are not the ones I'm talking about here. A truly genuine born-again Christian man will respect a woman. Also why I reiterate that you should keep out of unwedded sex, serious men do survey to see if a woman is serious. A Christian woman will have a lifestyle that will respect Christ. She is not worldly, she does not take into the nightclubs, alcohol, drugs, cigarettes, and all those secular forms of pleasure. She is truly born-again and allows the word of God to be her lead and guide. It is also her discernment. Being a serious born-again woman of God however does not qualify you to marry just anyone. You have to be married to a serious born-again man. So do not conclude that you accept a marriage proposal from a man who is not born-again simply because has proposed to you and he's handsome and is financially well up. Quit serving Satan! Even Satan likes good born-again brides so that he can enjoy terrorizing them in the future. And I vow to you when a woman who is truly born again and goes ahead and gets married to an un-Godly man the rest of her life will be a nightmare and her Christianity will remain highly compromised. As a young Christian woman, do not get tired of waiting for God. Do not let society pressurize you. Wait patiently for the right God-fearing man.

e) <u>Our dating and courtship:</u>

The following is an outline of our dating and courtship and it is our prayer that the Lord leads you to study it closely with the aim of emulating it as much as possible. Pray that the Lord leads you to a God-fearing man who will court you on a platonic path with the ultimate intention of walking you down the aisle in total holy matrimony.

1. Who Richard is

Richard has always been a praise and worship Assistant and at that time he was devoutly participating in 3 Church's praise and worship ministries. Richard's area of specialization is Keyboards, organ and Piano. He is also a music teacher. He graduated as B.A - Organ Major from the San Francisco Conservatory of Music.

2. Group dating:

We were always in church groups and had lots of couples who had been married many years. They served as role models within our church circles.

3. Our first valentine's day

Our first valentines day comprised of all married couples in fact we were the only dating couple in the whole church group. It was a pleasant Evening at the Marriot at San Ramon. This was on February 14th 2006. This Valentine's day dinner was organized by Richard's church.

4. Church functions and other functions that revolved around his music career

We prayed a lot together as a couple. In addition to regular church functions like services, bible-studies and fellowships, we also attended:

Church organized Picnics, barbeques, weddings:

We attended innumerable picnics, barbeques and weddings which were mainly during summer. Richard started playing for weddings since he was the age of 14. From the time I met him, I always accompanied him when he got contracted to play at these functions and still do so to date. It is a very entertaining and spiritually fulfilling life. Its not a wonder God blessed him with the kind of marriage he always desired. He had long sowed his seed. Of course as his fiancée I was always on the limelight whenever we appeared for these functions. Then I started meeting multitudes and multitudes of people known to Richard. Many-a-times when we are just around the Bay area going about our normal duties, so many people young and old would stop and just to greet Richard and they were either his old students, people he played for or people he went to church with. Remember that the Bay Area is a combination of mega-cities yet before the week was up at least 3 people would stop to greet Richard while I was his fiancée. Let society tell you what kind of man you are getting married to! If he had some dirt, the society would let it out! - I also accompanied him when he was contracted to play at funerals, usually from beginning to end. Funerals run throughout the year and for these too, I accompanied him. This highly educated me on the mode of conducting funerals here in America. I feel like it was some sort of training.

5. His eating habits

Preparing meals in my 2nd floor apartment where I lived and worked: We shared the apartment with my very dear workmate. I got into the habit of preparing him meals though we ate out from time to time. Usually after his meal, Richard would walk to his apartment, just 10 minute's walk away from mine. This was the time I realized that Richard loved to eat nice meals. So I came on board the marriage with that in mind.

6. How we met

I formally met Richard on January 16th 2006. It was a cold winter's evening. The lady who introduced us to each other prepared a dinner at her house. She & her husband are from East Africa, and they had met Richard many years ago since he was part of the Praise and worship ministry at the Church they attend. At one time, Richard confided in the couple - "if you know of a nice Christian woman from your Country, let me meet her, I would like to marry her". I'll call this lady Anna. She prepared a vegetarian dish. When I first set my eyes on Richard, it must have been God because I could deduce that he's a kind man. And one thing I can confess is that up to this day, my husbands kindness is consistent. There <u>is no day</u> he was mean to me. I was to confirm this through his mom when I later met his family. She told me that Richard is very unique among her children saying that none of her children can come close to Richard's level of kindness and gentleness. Sometimes when I examine myself, I find myself very rough. But I have been largely smoothened out by this marriage. When you get married to a kind man, you will also become gentle and kind. Some people say that I'm a giver. But no amount of giving and self-sacrifice can equal my husband's. This was a prayer answered because I don't know how I would have gotten along with a tight-fisted, mean husband.

7. He formally introduces me to his family

Within four months of meeting each other, in Easter 2006 (April), he drove me to San Bernardino

County to meet his family. They live about 400 miles from the Bay Area in a tiny city in San Bernardino County called Barstow very close to Las Vegas. Richard took me around to visit his old class-mates, and to visit all his old schools. He left for the Bay area when he was 18 years old. (He came out to join University in the Bay area and later settled and worked there). My parents-in-law are a lot like my own parents! They are a Christian family. My mom-in-law grows vegetables at her back-yard. There are also peach, fig, apricot and pear trees at the back-yard. Summers are hmmmm!! mum sends us fruit from her back yard all the way to Oakland by post. My family in Kenya is also Christian, my mom has a vegetable garden and when I was in boarding school, my mum always sent me cookies and candy by post! Richard's parents are a lot like my parents. When we went to Barstow, I took this time to learn to make as many American dishes as I could. Sunday was a church day and the local town was pleased to learn that Richard was in town. He played at the church where his dad is a member of the choir. My mom-in-law serves in the church as a Eucharistic minister, taking communion to church members who are unable to come to church due to home-ridden illnesses. I also got a time to meet all his brothers, sisters and their families. It was during this visit to his home that I mentioned that my parents would like to meet Richard and his parents before we wedded.

8. Our engagement:

By July 2006, he engaged me with a beautiful gold ring with tiny mounted diamonds. We also set up a web-page informing all our friends and family at home and abroad - of our engagement and imminent holy matrimony. The web-page contained information on both of us quoting the following:

Richard: Born-again Christian since Summer 1984; Has led a God-fearing life, has never been married and has no children. His career: Music teacher and a praise and worship assistant at his church.

Winnie: Born again Christian since March 12th 1993. Has led a God-fearing life, has never been married and has no children. Career: French teacher & caregiver.

We began marriage counseling sessions by Pastor Butler, who was my Pastor at the Love Fellowship COGIC (Church of God in Christ) where I was a member for 6 years. He was later to officiate our wedding in Summer the following year. Usually by secular standards, couples who are engaged went ahead and had a sexual life. But our engagement and dating were purely platonic. Like never before, even our Pastor saw to it that he would only recognize purity. Pastor Butler has a long standing career during which he has joined many couples in holy matrimony, having done so for over 30 years. His method of counseling has proven viable and that's why most couples he joined are still married after very many years. Pre-marital counseling is not the only service he offers. Also offered along with this therapy is post-marital counseling.

9. Richard and his mother travel to Nyeri, Kenya.

They took the trip to specifically ask for my hand in marriage according to the Christian Kikuyu customs. This took place in October 2006. They flew to Kenya by KLM Royal Dutch Airlines from San Francisco International Airport through Amsterdam.

My green-card had not yet come through, so it was not possibly safe to travel. But since my family had spoken frequently to the Rileys by phone and had exchanged lots of photos, when they finally met at the Jomo Kenyatta International airport in Nairobi, they felt like they had always known each other. The flight was the longest any of them had ever taken. They formally met my parents and all my relatives to ask for my hand in marriage. In Kenya, I come from the *kikuyu tribe*. There was a big ceremony called: *uthoni* which is the *kikuyu* traditional wedding. The groom declares to the elders the purpose of his visit. Richard did not really know what to expect. So I explained to him that there would be a big gathering of friends and relatives. He would be required to address them and explain to them the purpose of his visit. So all this time, he was getting ready with a small speech. He inquired of me: What if they do not accept? And I told him "Man, you better be neat because if they say no, then that's the end". That is because, in proper *kikuyu* custom, parents are highly respected and their word taken seriously when it comes to choosing a marriage partner. So actually in black and white I would say that I was confident that they would like Richard - and I mentioned that to him. Also in Kikuyu custom, a bride is not given to the groom. The person to whom the bride is handed over is the parent/s of the boy. So in this respect, the Rileys were well prepared. The ceremony itself was beautiful and highly festive. There were about 70 invited guests and my parents were especially happy that guests from the USA would honor their culture by coming physically and asking for the hand of their daughter in marriage. Richard's speech centered around how he had met me, and most of all, he stressed that he is looking forward to having Christ as the center of our marriage. He also declared to them that he thanked God that he'd found himself the proverbs 31 woman. After Richard's request was consented, there was a lot of dancing and feasting. Richard's mom also gave a small speech. The crowd then danced to *kikuyu* and *kiswahili* Christian music. There was a lot of Kenyan food too. Also to join Richard in this festive dance was my late paternal grandmother whom I'm named after according to the kikuyu naming traditions. Let me mention that concerning my aunts and uncles - both paternal and maternal, marriage has a very strong covenant. All my paternal aunties and uncles married properly in church and had white weddings except for one uncle who is now deceased. On my mother's side, all my aunties and uncles married properly in church and had white weddings except one auntie who is a born-again spirit-filled avowed spinster. There have also been some nasty divorces on my maternal side of the family because as you know, life is not always a smooth path. These too have provided me with a profound learning experience. In spite of all this, we are a family that predominantly honors the marriage covenant. I did not wish to be the one to break the pattern. Over and above honoring our cultural traditions, the real driving force behind seeking parental consent was being God-fearing Christians who take the word of God seriously. According to the 10 Commandments in Exodus 20 v 12: **"Honour thy father and thy mother: that thy days may be long upon the land which the Lord thy God giveth thee."**

As we are all aware, this is the only command with Promise. We did not want to miss out of that blessing and as we all know the future is waiting for us. We would like our children to seek our counsel in marital decisions.

<u>Nov 2006</u>: Richard flies back home from Kenya a highly exited man that my family had consented to our relationship and we were allowed to go ahead with our wedding preparations. We set our wedding for August 25th 2007 because it was going to be high-summer. We set that time so that we could have ample time for the preparations. It also gave friends and family time to prepare themselves. 6 relatives flew in from Kenya purposely for this wedding. Lots of family and friends flew in to California from out-of-state.

August 25th 2007: We wedded after one year and eight months of courtship.

10. Time: a crucial factor in the quest to evaluate a life-partner.

I first heard of Richard in December 2005, but it was not until January 16th 2006 that I got to physically meet him. The Lord had kept my future husband safe and ordained the time and place I would meet him. But as you know, when God is about to send you a husband, the devil too has his counterfeit and he's ready to hurl him at you. Our courtship lasted one year and eight months. I would advice couples intending to marry to give each other time. I do hear some marriage counselors advising two years. But in principle, allow enough time, long enough that both of you will have their characteristics fully come to the surface before you get married. For sure you know, a man cannot pretend for a prolonged length of time. I would, out of my own experience, have 3 aspects that would only unravel and come out in clear perspective only when given ample time when trying to evaluate that OWM.

a) A man's sexual habits and his faithfulness to you:

Our entire courtship was purely platonic. This was what we always learnt at home and at church throughout our entire lives. A great influence in my life was my paternal auntie Cate Ngala who lived with us and is 8 years older than myself. She was the big-sister figure in my life. So she started dating long before myself. She advised me to keep dating platonic so that I would be left to observe if a man will go searching for sex elsewhere. If he does, good! Just helps quicken your elimination process and move on to the next one. If he keeps you in full focus of his intent over a period of more than 1 1/2 years, it shows that he's sexually behaved and he can control his body and this shows that he has sexual integrity. This is also a good test because he will stay with you and enjoy being with you and still cherish your other qualities in the absence of sex. Those men who leave you because you cannot provide sex in courtship only prove that it's the only thing they were looking out for and they'll get it elsewhere. Again, let them go!!

If a man sneaks behind you and gets some sex outside your courtship and still intends to marry you, it shows that he'll do the same even when you are married to him. I have some bad news for you: Be ready to share him with other women even when he marries you. Some women have no way of recognizing when a man is being deceptive in a relationship. Here are some pointers: Not giving you his home telephone number; Not introducing you to family and friends and not accepting to meet yours; Declining to say where he lives; Having too many secrets eg, where he works etc. A Christian man should be transparent enough to invite you to his church because marriage is legal and public. If he tries to make your relationship private, just know this relationship has no roots, it will soon crumble.

b) *Personal habits*

You will need to know a man long enough in order to determine if you will accept those personal traits which you cannot possibly change. Do not let marriage catch you by surprise. Time in courtship allows you the woman and man to learn each other's personal habits: Feeding habits, financial habits, etc. For example, I learnt that Richard loves to eat well. So during our courtship I had to learn to fix good dishes because gourmet cooking is also one of my hobbies. I had my mom-in-law and the ladies in my church teach me to cook as many American dishes as possible. Up to today, food is a top priority in our home.

I also learnt that Richard is a hard worker though not as highly organized with finances as myself. So that helped us streamline a financial strategy long before we got married. And needless to say, finances form a very crucial part of not just married life, but life in general. And for sure, you need a lot of time to study a person's financial habits in order to come up with a workable plan of action once the marriage takes route. You have to pray very hard, because agreeing on financial matters takes God. We thank God that due to the time we had dedicated to our courtship, by the time we were planning our wedding we had a workable and harmonious financial plan of action. One aspect that saw Richard's financial habits not well rooted was that in spite of being a good Christian man, he was not a regular tither. This is a problem with many Christians all over the world. They are worshipping God, but not fully trusting him with their finances. By God's grace, Richard came fully on board and as you know, tithing secures all manner of finances and yields a strong financial harvest be it on an individual basis, a married couple, a business or any form of entity:

Malachi 3: 8 - 10 "Will a man rob God? Yet ye have robbed me. But ye say, wherein have we robbed thee? In tithes and offerings. Bring ye all the tithes into the storehouse, that there may be meat in mine house, and prove me now herewith, saith the Lord of hosts, if I will not open you the windows of heaven and pour you out a blessing, that there shall not be room enough to receive it........." Touching on tithing, it is the only area that God commands us to test him!

c) *Spiritual edification:*

Being a praise and worship Assistant at his church, I became more inclined to Richard's ministry. Before we got married, I found myself begin to sing at church occasions and I gained full momentum once we got married. I got to learn more and more about music. More enriching still were our telephone conversations at the end of each day during our courtship. When we both got back to our respective homes, we would talk on the phone for long hours usually to the early morning hours! Many times we said to each other "I cannot believe I'm this blessed!" We constantly marveled at the great things God was doing for us. And the word of God is reminding us that discussing him is not a vain thing:

Malachi 3: 16 - 18 is telling us great things "Then they that feared the Lord spake often to one another: and the Lord harkened and heard it and a book of remembrance was written before him for them that feared the Lord, and thought upon his name. <u>And they shall be mine, saith the Lord of hosts, in that day when I make up my jewels and I will spare them as a man spareth his own son that serveth him. And then shall ye return, and discern between the righteous and the wicked, between him that serveth God and him that serveth him not.</u>"

It is no wonder God promises a beautiful life if we place him first in our lives and confess him both privately and publicly.

RICHARD'S VIEWS

Richard's views and the qualities he was looking out for in a wife:

He starts by saying "I thank the Lord that I found myself the proverbs 31 woman........"

In Richard's view, he desired a wife who was not only a Christian, but a committed one and one who does not compromise with the world in any way. Another quality he required was kindness and that she too had to be a one-man's-woman. The funny thing is that I did not know all along what qualities he was looking for. I just happened to write down those qualities as I write this book. This is a paragraph dedicated to Richard's contribution, this is the first time I'm coming in touch with his side of the story. It is as new to me as it is to you!

CHAPTER 2

a) <u>Obedience to God:</u>

One thing I wish to advice you ladies is that OWM are extremely rare to find and let's cry to God to release them to us. The one language that the Lord will understand is <u>OUR OBEDIENCE</u> to him as women. Let's do what the Lord says and like a good student who does all their homework and carries out the instructions of his/her teachers, it is the same with God. He sets rules for you, just follow them. If you follow them right, you will be rewarded. If you compromise, you will have a compromised result. The choice is yours!

Let's look at the words of:

Psalms 119: 89 - 96 (*LAMED*) "For ever O Lord, thy word is settled in heaven. Thy faithfulness is unto all generations; thou hast established the earth and it abideth. They continue this day according to thine ordinances: for all are thy servants. Unless thy law had been my delights, I should then have perished in mine affliction. I will never forget thy precepts: for with them thou hast quickened me. I am thine, save me; for I have sought thy precepts. The wicked have waited for me to destroy me: but I will consider thy testimonies. I have see an end of all perfection: but thy commandment is exceeding broad"

The funny thing is that we are living in an age where everything is simplified for us especially here in the USA. Oh yes! when you want to pay a bill, you just do it electronically; when you want to drive from point a to b, you just get your GPS or map-quest! Some pastors have also gotten into this trend and are trying to also simplify Christianity by trying to make our walk with God 'user-friendly', and they proceed on to preaching to their congregations not to worry because we will be saved on account of grace and not of works. The effect of this on congregations is implied complacency because preachers are not consistent on giving them that vital drive to be Christ-like. Living according to the standards of God will never be on-line and we will not be e-ticketed to heaven. Hey!! there are no short-cuts. Read the bible for yourself and do not let any pastors mislead you:

17. James 2: 24 "Ye see then now that by works a man is justified and not by faith only."

- v26:" For as the body without the spirit is dead, so faith without works is dead also.

- V17 - 18:"Even so faith, if it hath not works is dead being alone. Yea, a man may say, Thou hast faith and I have works: shew me thy faith without thy works, and I will shew thee my faith by my works"

18. Matthew 5 v 17: "Think not that I come to destroy the law, or the prophets: I am not come to destroy but to fulfil"

If you are a God-fearing, morally upright, young woman, dwell in the word of God and the OWM will marry you with no hesitation.

b) <u>What does a OWM look for in a wife</u>?

Proverbs 31 woman. About the women in the bible with an anointing for marriage:Hannah, Sarah, Ruth, the Shunammite woman of 2nd Kings Ch: 4, Mary, Elizabeth, Esther. These women have one quality in common - they had such a strong anointing for marriage, so strong that when they got married, their marriages lasted and they were a pride to their husbands who simply would not let go of them. They remained in marriage even when some among them were unable to bear children. Pray for God to endow you with the anointing for marriage he accorded to these great wives of the bible.

c) <u>Do not get involved with a disputed man, or unequally yoked men.</u>

Trying to change an unequally yoked man is a vain effort and you'll end up losing your salvation.

As you know, it is easier to drop from a tree than it is to climb up one. And we know that when you lose your salvation, you are DONE! A disputed man will gravitate towards another woman mainly as an escape route from a problematic marriage. The main driving force is lust. Other driving forces include adventure and escape. Out of observing society, it is a fact that these men do so habitually. As a woman, do not suppose that you are any special. These men have seasonal habits. They have a season to take on a woman and a season to dump her. Concerning his wife, her time to be dumped has come and its now time for him to pick another woman and that happens to be you! And when the circle comes to full completion, you will be the current woman in his life and then your season to be dumped is imminent. Its just a question of time. The third part of the cycle is to reconcile with the woman they dumped last - usually because of ties eg children and property. That is why in America, as in many parts of the world, you will see a man who has children with two, three, four, even up to six different women! And each time he is with any of them, he'll just complain to his current woman "oh! its my baby's mama". And when he goes over to "see his children" you have no business questioning what relationship they had and what they did while they were together. This disputed man will play circus with his women and the women will be bickering all over. But the fact is that the problem is with the man. A disputed man can never be a OWM because a OWM loves only one woman and the love is genuine. So you cannot explain how a man can love more than one woman in a lifetime while they are all alive. It is not possible for a man to love two women simultaneously.

Women who are married to disputed men will just not disclose it to you: that it is "hell".

You are not to be divorced except on grounds of adultery. This qualifies you to remarry. **Matthew 5 v 32 "But I say unto you, That whosoever shall put away his wife, saving for the cause of fornication, causeth her to commit adultery"** The other once-married man/woman who you can also marry in accordance to the word of God is a widower/widow - and let it not be an HIV-Aids widower/widow for goodness sake!!

So the fact that a man is damping a woman for you should not make you think that you are special. Think twice. And single women, if you want to experiment on this one, go ahead. You will be your own good example of being degraded by a non-believer because you are just being used as a fire-quencher.

The bible is clearly telling us in **2nd Corinthians Ch 6 V 14 - 17: "Be ye not unequally yoked together with unbelievers: for what fellowship hath righteousness with unrighteousness? and what communion hath light with darkness? But what concord hath Christ with Belial? or what part hath he that believeth with an infidel? And what agreement hath the temple of God with idols? for ye are the temple of the living God; as God hath said, I will dwell in them, and walk in them; and I will be their God and they shall be my people. Wherefore come out from among them, and be ye separate, saith the Lord..."**

One born-again woman was trying to convince her Pastor that she needed to be wedded to this man even though he was not born-again. Reason being........ "just because she loved him" saying: "You know pastor, ...Love covers a multitude of sin". I would like to warn you that marriage is not the place to play gymnastics with scripture seeking to have them suit your fleshly motives....Quit using the bible as a dictionary and begin honoring it as the infallible word of God!!.

I know that many Christians go through the phase of trying to convert a non-born-again person with the intention to marry them. Please stop! Women! if a man is not born-again, let your journey end there. Do not consider him for marriage. I will give my own example of a friendship I had with a man from Togo in 2004 right where I live in the Bay area of California. I met him at a friend's barbeque in August 2004. My friend had thrown a barbeque in honor of her mother who was visiting from Kenya. The barbeque was in Fremont. It was at this time that this Togolese man approached me. I will call him Willy though, of course, this is not his real name. What led me to feel convinced that this man was highly attracted to me was because throughout the barbeque, he never left my side. I was there in the company of a friend of mine who had requested me to accompany her there. When I got to the party, I was rather alone and that's when I saw this man just come and sit next to me. He was not talking much. Each time I finished eating, he would offer to pick more food for me. He only gathered to speak to me about one hour before we left. Throughout that one hour, I learnt that he was five years younger than I, and that he was Togolese. He did not seem to mind the age difference. In my single life, I noticed that younger men were repeatedly attracted to me. It could be due to my small body structure that highly conceals the reality of my age. He marveled that I spoke French and since his English was not very fluent, he was only relieved that we could converse in French. He had the most lovely demeanor. He was soft spoken, polite and had perfect manners he also spoke very decently and I mentioned to him that I was a born-again Christian. He then informed me that he likes to go to Church. That is a good starting point! I said to myself. He asked me for my telephone number. By the time I reached home, he had called me twice. The following day, he woke me up with a phone call, we had a conversation and I realized that he was known to some Togolese friends of mine. I asked him about his relationship with Christ and he told me that he loved God. This was a Monday. So I invited him to church the following Sunday, but he declined saying that he had to go to work. He worked at Target and he was also pursuing studies in the field of pharmacy. So he worked and went to school and this is usually very hard. But he kept calling. He could even call me in early morning hours like 2.00am. He also cooked very well so he told me of the dishes he likes to fix. He never invited me to visit him even once, not even for an outing like a dinner. In mind I decided just to learn more about him with the hope that I may bring Christ into his life. In our conversations, I learnt that he neither drunk nor smoked he was also struggling financially due to his work/school situation. So I decided to take the initiative and invited him over. This was in September 2004. We arranged that he visit me on a Sunday so that we could go to church first and then later we could have lunch at my place. Again the fact that he was struggling financially with work and studies caused me to be compassionate in my heart, and this caused me to overlook the fact that he never invited me out. So I ran the extra mile and told him I would fix lunch at my place after church. By a month's time in our friendship, he mentioned sex a few times and I told myself, "I'll preach to him till he knows that pre-marital sex is a sin". We went to church and I could see by his church participation that he was not a habitual church goer. He however gave offering and gave me some money to give as an offering too. And I told myself, yes Jesus! he is honoring you with his substance! When we went home after church, my room-mate was home and I introduced Willy to her. We all ate lunch and had a good time, enjoyed talking and sharing life experiences. By the time he left, he did not mention when next he needed to see me. But immediately he got home, the showers of phone calls started again. Sometimes calling even six or seven times in a day. From this time on, he mentioned love and marriage. Again I told myself, "by the time he completes college, he will be born-again and we can get married." He hinted about sex from time to time and I said in my spirit "the Devil is a liar, this man will be saved and because he is so nice, he just needs the Lord". I gave him God's word regarding sex and he agreed with me that pre-marital sex is a sin. I did mention to him that I would be having an out-patient surgical procedure in a month's time, a biopsy to remove a lump in my breast. He did not mention anything of importance to that effect. He kept calling and I kept saying in my heart, "I will win him for Jesus". I also mentioned to him that my birthday would be coming in early October. On the d-day, he called me at mid-night and was actually the first person to wish me a happy birthday. I was so impressed!! My employer who was in the habit of taking me out for my birthday took me out to the Emeryville mall for lunch. On our way back, she asked me "How about your friend from Togo, did he call you? where is he taking you for your birthday?" I was happy to mention that he was the first to wish me a happy birthday, but I had no answer for the second question. And it remained that way. Willy never called me until after 2 days. When he finally called and asked what I was doing, I informed him that I was just in the house just relaxing. For the second time, I informed him that I would be having out-patient surgery in November. He never commented. I even informed him of my appointments with the doctor and all the surgical paperwork that I had to do. All this time, I had said in my mind, "oh, Willy will be there". So for this reason, I decided not to bother my friends. It was a tag-of-war in my mind - because he said severally that he loved me and I was positive that he would be at least kind enough to see me through surgery.

A week to surgery, he stopped calling. I felt a bit depressed. But I asked God to take control.

Everyone I knew was busy at work and at short notice, I realized that I had no-one to fetch me from out-patient surgery and I needed help because I was to be put under general anesthesia. I prayed to God and he told me to be bold, and bold I was. I did not call, I was waiting for his full traits to emerge. On the day of surgery, I called a close friend Evangelist Suzzane Njuguna of the King Jesus ministry. She volunteered to be there with me throughout surgery and take me home afterwards. That was God. I knew that God loved me that a woman this senior in ministry could put her time aside for me.

After recovering, I did not call Willy and he called about a week after surgery. At that time, my house phone did not have caller ID so I just picked calls without knowing the caller. By the first week of December, I was fully recovered and back to work. By the time Willy called, in my opinion, it was a very bad joke. Our conversation went something like this: "how have you been?" and I replied ok. "How is work?" and I replied ok. So I expressly asked him why he kept off communication during and after surgery. To this he replied "Oh!, I never knew you needed my help". To this I just told him ok, and good-bye. He pleaded with me not to disconnect the phone and so I asked him to say what he had to say because I was busy. He said "I was calling to say that I love you, I'm sorry that I did not come to see you and I would like to come and spend the night at your place". I told him "You mention that you would like to spend the night at my house?" and he replied "Yes!" and I went on further to say "That sounds like a valid idea, but in who's house do you want to spend the night?" and he replied "in your house". And I asked him "to spend the night in my house as who and in the name of what??" He just burst out sobbing and crying. I could hear him crying out loudly from the other side. From then on I put a caller ID on my phone and never picked his calls again.

Ladies, that was a waste of 5 months of my single life: Trying to convert a non-believer with the hope that he can marry me! I would advice every God-fearing, born-again Christian woman to just ignore any form of relationship with a man who is not born-again. In fact, meeting such a man is a blessing from God because the mere fact that he lacks a testimony is an indicator that Jesus is not resident in his heart. It helps you with the elimination process very fast and opens up new options very fast. Remember that the enemy is very subtle and he sends the non-Christian men to waste your time and as women, you know what time means. Satan's other intent is that you ultimately fall into the sexual sin.

d) Secular media

The media has highly impacted the sexual revolution that has given people the worldly image of sexuality, totally contrary to the word of God. And when this happens, the marriage and the family remain targets of the enemy. You can unknowingly worship Satan just by the music you listen to. Please recall that Satan took music, God's instrument of praise and turned it around to be an instrument to praise himself. Television, and the worldly standards all come to challenge and influence the way you relate to men. Marriage, the secular media implies, is done as a result of a thing we call 'love' that has actually come to be defined as a 'feeling'. But in reality, marriage is a covenant. You can only make a covenant with either God or Satan. This is well laid out in the book of Genesis and in Ephesians 5. If you make it with God, it will be a peaceful, fulfilling one. If you make it with Satan, it will never give you peace. That's why worldly marriages talk of a man who loves two or three women simultaneously. That is of the devil himself. This is because Satan is trying to destroy the couple in the guise of giving them extra-marital escapades. If you are to live a Godly life, quit every form of worldly media that contradicts the word of God. If you think Christianity is boring, then I assure you that a non-Christian life is tormenting and of course Christianity is not boring. Just try it. And if you doubt it, go to Satan's world. It will wear you down and you will have no peace. If you are to entertain yourself, keep to the entertainment that has God-friendly themes: music, movies, television. Media and music dealing with violence, pornography, lust and sexual adventures all underlying the rampant theme of deception all belong to their father the devil:

John 8:44 "Ye are of your father the devil, and the lusts of your father you will do. He was a murderer from the beginning, and abode not in the truth, because there is no truth in him. When he speaketh a lie, he speaketh of his own: for he is a liar and the father of it."

Most of these women in the worldly media engage in such strong power-play with their antagonists, you cannot help but identify the spirit of the woman Jezebelle. And of course you know that no OWM wants a Jezebelle for a wife because this type of woman is promiscuous and this spirit will always come to haunt the marriage. You can read about this evil woman in the book of 1st Kings.

e) Occupy your time socializing with God-fearing women who are successfully married.

I. Suzzane Njuguna, Evangelist of The King Jesus Ministry: This great woman of God is my mentor. I was her protégée and about four years before I met my husband, she gave me what I would define as a crush-course that prepared me for marriage. By then, I was headed to my mid-thirties. She was also a source of comfort, assuring me that if I kept to the word of God, he would be impressed and consequently release that good Christian man to my life because according to her and her husband Pastor Booker.T.Randon: "God has many nice men in his kingdom and he can gladly release one of them to you".

Suzzane is also the author of "A voice in the midst of the storm", also published by Xulon Publishers Inc. in Florida USA.

Sowing seeds and tithing: I sowed a very handsome amount of money as seed in King Jesus Ministry because it is a Ministry that has a strong anointing for Marriage. Sowing seed is bibilical and the following is scripture to support this:

2 Corinthians 9: v 8 - 13 "God is able to make all grace abound toward you; that ye always having all sufficiency in all things, may abound to every good work: As it is written, he hath dispersed abroad; he hath given to the poor: his righteousness remaineth for ever. Now he that ministereth seed to the sower both minister bread for your food, and multiply your seed sown, and increase the fruits of your righteousness. Being enriched in every thing to all bountifulness, which causeth through us thanksgiving to God. For the administration of this service not only supplieth the

want of saints but is abundant also by many thanksgivings to God. Whiles by the experiment of this ministration they glorify God for your professed subjection unto the gospel of Christ, and for your liberal distribution unto them and unto all men."

My maternal auntie Carol Gateere always taught me how to sow seed. I have lived a life of sowing seed for practically every blessing I need from God. I learnt to sow seed when I became a delivered Christian in 1997. Be it a job, or just any real blessing that I needed from the Lord. And one way to sow seed is to sow it on fertile ground where there is anointing for that particular blessing you are seeking. So one day Auntie Carol asked me: "have you considered sowing seed for a husband?" and sure enough I hadn't. So I went into prayer in May

2004. By the end of that month, the Lord directed me to sow in King Jesus Ministry that is directed by Pastor Booker T Randon and his wife Suzzane Njuguna. By then I had been a part of this ministry (now based in Texas), which had weekly televised broadcasts in the Bay Area of California. Suzzane used to teach me about being a Godly wife. She actually prepared me for marriage long before I was married. So when I sowed a very handsome amount of money and named it "my husband", I knew that God had to work something. Suzzane is a great intercessor and she took me up as a spiritual daughter. Within one and a half years of working closely with her, I met the man who was to be my husband. But before then, the enemy also gave me his counterfeit. Suzzane warned me "By the time that God will be ready to send a husband your way, be sure that Satan, the enemy will also send his counterfeit!". The same month that I was to meet my husband Richard, I was introduced to a Kenyan man, a very good-looking tall man who professed the word of God though he was not born-again. I will call him Eric. He met me in November 2005. He spoke of wedding me in February 2006. We used to take walks in the park, and talk for long hours over the phone. He never once invited me to his church. But I told myself: this man is decent. And he promises marriage because he made me believe that he had found in me a good Christian woman. I invited him to my church once, he met my pastor and other leaders of my church. We even went together for the friends and family fellowship - which is a dinner that my church hosted from time to time. All my pastor said is that "we should give it time". What convinced me that this man was suitable was because he was from Kenya like myself!!! So I knew that I was ok!

He was however not introducing me to his family members and I started smelling a rat. But since he spoke of marriage a lot, I knew that I had nothing to fear and within a short while, we would be married. He informed me that when we got married, we would be living in Livermore. I wondered why he suggested that we live so far away.

At the end of Dec 2005, I went away to visit a friend of mine for a week. She lives in a different part of California. I'll call her Terry, though not her real name. I requested to be away from Eric for a week to which he consented, and I left knowing that I had his blessings.

I traveled to my friend's city and on arrival found out that Terry's mum who was also visiting at the time had postponed going back to her home because she needed to spend more time with her daughter. This turned out to be times of prayer for all the things that were going on in our lives. God is faithful because He answered all that we had prayed for. I called Eric to inform him of my arrival. I also informed Terry's mom about my relationship with Eric. I'll call Terry's mom Ruth, though not her real name. Upon informing Ruth of my relationship with Eric, she subsequently spoke to him on the phone. She gave me a good report saying that she believed the man was nice. She mentioned that he impressed her because he spoke with a lot of respect. She however advised me to give it time. Ruth is a woman to reckon with because she is a good wife, a great mother of many children both biological and adoptive. In addition to this she holds a long standing career as a leader for the advancement of women in Kenya and internationally.

By the second day Eric had not called. So I called severally both on his house phone and his cell-phone but could not reach him. The following day, I called a lady we knew in common and asked her if she had seen Eric. She informed me that she had seen him in church and that he was in the company of another woman. I really stressed out. By the end of the week, he had not called me. On the day I was due back to Oakland, He called me and requested to know my time of arrival. He had not spoken to me all this time and here he was asking me what time I was due back. I informed him that I would be in Oakland at 4.00pm. He did not turn up to meet me. So I arrived home sad and exhausted and wondering what next. This was the time I prayed. I prayed many times with my prayer partners and asked for God's directions. I also decided not to call him. He stayed 2 days without calling. When he finally did call, he accused me saying that I gave all my time to my friends and that I'm too social. I felt offended though I did not tell him. I prayed like never before.

My friend Rosa (not her real name) also informed me again that he was seen again with this lady and it there was evidence that it was a physical relationship. It really broke my insides. Rosa is born-again and a great friend of mine she and her husband are from East Africa. She is happily married and serves as a deacon in her church. Then Rosa told me not to worry, but to pray. She saw my anguish and informed me that there is a single African-American man who has been in the praise and worship ministry in her church for very many years. At one time, this man mentioned to her that if she knew of any nice, born-again Christian lady from her country, she should introduce her to him. So bearing this in mind, Rosa told me not to worry, she would introduce me to Richard. She made a dinner at her house and invited both of us. It was at this Dinner that I met my future husband. From then on, everything flowed smoothly. There was no disappointment, there was no period of silence in our relationship and everything flowed smoothly. We prayed together a lot and we attended church functions together. He never hid anything from me, I felt one with him. We also shared scripture and spoke for long hours on the phone. What was exemplary at the beginning of what was to be a courtship was that we spent all our leisure time together. When we were both not working, we spent that time together. This is evidence of a blessed courtship. In the meantime, Eric called me within the first week of meeting Richard and asked me why I was not communicating with him. I informed him that I was in prayer for God to give him a wife. He could not believe that I had left him. Of course I did not mention anything about meeting Richard. I did not want to be the one to hit him with that blow. I wanted him to learn it through other sources. I informed him that I wished him the best. He did not stop calling. At one time he asked me if I had met someone else and this time I had to own up. This affirmation broke his heart. I asked him to stop calling. I kindly requested him to be civil because I did not want to block his number from my phones. I asked him to peacefully stop calling and this way we could part ways in peace without intruding into each other's privacy. In the meantime I spoke to Richard about Eric and we started praying that Eric meets a nice woman whom he would marry. We prayed for him for about a year and by God's grace, he met a nice lady and he's now married. So ladies, be careful not to get deceived by the enemy into marrying in a hurry and marrying the devil's choice. In his marriage Eric is not faithful to his wife. He is known for having girlfriends on the side. This is what I would have gotten myself into. I would have been married to a man who was promiscuous. And that's why he wanted to marry me because he knew that I did not have sexual sin, but keep his girlfriends on the side! Beware not to marry the devil's counterfeit. Suzanne had warned me about this man. She knew of his personal life and was conversant with the life he led and so she advised me that he would not make a good husband. And since you know that the devil comes to steal our time, I stayed on the friendship with Eric, just long enough to prove that Suzanne was right.

Listen to the prophets of God! Surround yourselves with God fearing women! I prayed fervently for many days. In my distress, the Lord gave me this scripture: **Isaiah 59 v 19: ".... So shall they fear the name of the Lord from the west and his glory from the rising of the sun. <u>When the enemy shall</u>**

come in like a flood, the spirit of the Lord will lift up a standard against him".

When the enemy came upon me with a counterfeit, I cried to the Lord and he raised up a standard and revealed my husband to me. Praise be to God!! AMEN.

II. Teresa: Just the two of us used to do street evangelism and witnessing and we started on November 29th 2004. We continued in this ministry at Hayward Bart station and South Hayward Bart station in the East Bay of California. Little did I know that God was to bless me through this great woman of God. It is through her that I physically met my husband. She is the woman who spoke to every God-fearing woman she met and she asked them: "I have a very dear sister and she's God fearing and she's trusting God for a Born-again husband. Do you know any such man of God?..... my sister can make a perfect

God-fearing wife. She has been receiving marriage proposals from worldly men and she has no intention of covenanting with any of them. Do you know any brother who needs a serious Christian wife?". She is the one who connected me to Rosa.

This leads us to the next most important aspect:

f) THE DOS AND DONT'S OF A CHRISTIAN WOMAN

i) Decline hasty engagements, say a big no! (Also see Ch 1 no. d 10(ten)

When a man tries to marry you in a hurry, just trust your senses and be advised that something is amiss. There is something he is trying to hide from you and he's aware that if you discover early, you would turn him down. But he sees that you can make a good wife and so he marries you in a hurry, probably impregnates you and then you are stuck!! moving will be another milestone around your neck. If a man is willing to marry you, let him give you time so that you can both study each other!!

The Christian woman does not hurry to get married. She does not participate in the fairly-tale love at first sight affair that sweeps you off your feet and carries you to your prince charming. The Christian woman who is in search of a OWM is careful: time and caution are her most treasured tools.

Immediately after I completed my education at Kenyatta University with a B.Ed(Hons) degree, I proceeded to Paris, France where I joined L' Institut Catholique de Paris and underwent a study of the French Press system. It was a brief course. During this time, I had a part-time job both at the Kenyan Permanent Delegation to UNESCO and the Kenya Tourist Office (KTO). I mainly did bilingual duties

(French/English) which included translation, word-processing and front-desk duties according to the current projects of these two offices. I was 23 years of age, very young and actually very fresh in the employment arena. It was however not my first time to be in France. It is a country on which my entire study was centered and I had been there in the Summer of 1989 taking part in a language familiarization program and staying with a French family as a *jeune-fille-au-pair* prior to completing my bachelor's degree at Kenyatta University in Kenya.

Though I used to attend the American Church in Paris, I was not a born-again Christian. I'm sure the world knows how much champagne flows in the streets of Paris; and that wine is cheaper than water in France. Yes, I enjoyed it all in my student days. I also liked partying at City Rock and going to the all the small joints at St. Michel. As students we used to host a lot of house parties and no weekend passed without a party somewhere. When I compared these days with my student days at Kenyatta University, I realized that I was surely going wild. One thing I vividly remembered was that I never found joy in any of these things. I was always hurting. By God's grace, I completed my studies at L'Institut Catholique de Paris. Of course those days in Europe, Immigration was a real issue. Work permits did not come by easily for immigrants of African origin and even the part-time jobs we did as students were based on our student visas. So I found myself on my way back home after my studies. There was this man I had briefly met. He was French and 30 years old at the time. I will call him Etienne. He virtually begged me to marry him. I met him through a South African friend of mine who was a classmate at L'Institut Catholique de Paris. That just didn't sound right.

Me? Marry who? No! my total being was rejecting the whole thing. He was a very generous man, always showered me with gifts, but something did'nt feel right. At 23, the last thing on my mind was marriage. I was nowhere near there. Even though I had previously met my high-school sweet-heart whom I dearly loved and even contemplated being his wife, I just didn't picture myself married to Etienne. And I kept my motto: no pre-marital sex! And something about France just did not feel right. Then came the whole immigration crisis when the only way to get *'la carte blanche'* (the French equivalent of an American Green-Card) was only by being married to a French citizen. Then Etienne mentioned that to me as though to remind me. I rather he didn't. I virtually ran away from France. Back in home in Kenya, I recalled just how dark life was in France, how Etienne loved listening to Requiem music, and loved visiting cemeteries, watching horror movies and so many other dingy things that he used to do. My insides cried NO!! I totally accepted the fact that it was not God's purpose for me to live in France for the rest of my life. I consequently left for Kenya, my birth-country. While in Kenya, life was hard. I connected with my former college-mates, most of whom were already in the job market. For me, life was financially hard because reasonable Jobs were rare to come by, and I found myself being contracted to work on part-time basis most of the time. I depended on my parents for a long time before I could get reasonably employed. I enjoyed going out to the discos and eating out with former college-mates. At this time, I was simultaneously drawing close to God. If I spent a week going out to the clubs, I would make sure that Sunday found me at Church. One group of former classmates liked meeting at a place we called 'lips' on *Moi avenue*. This was early 1993. If it was not lips it was "bubbles", and if not "bubbles", it was "the visions". The list went on and on. In all this life of hanging out, I was not what you could call a typical drinker. I just used to sip wine with my friends as a way of socializing. I was also very protective of my body and still virgin. I never allowed men to play around with me. But on my return home to Kenya in late 1992, I met a man from the group of friends I hanged out with. He liked hanging out with them. Something in common with this group is that they were all *wakamba (From the Akamba community)*. This man had a liking for me. He kept telling me that we should get married. But he had a big problem, he drunk like a fish, and he was a party animal. But I told myself, if I got married to this man, he would drown me with his drinking. Actually one big reason for partying was that I tremendously loved to dance. We'll call him Steve (Though it is not his real name). My friends had mentioned to me that he had a girlfriend. But he never appeared with her on our parties. And when I confronted him about it, he denied of her existence. One time in January 1993, the group decided that we would have a party at his house in Lower Kabete. We bought the food that we would prepare and the drinks that we would take. Then we all met at his place, we were a group of about six of us and amongst us one couple. At his house we saw this lady who was always so busy in the kitchen, fixing food and cleaning. And then one lady among us sneaked up to me and whispered to me that it was Steve's girlfriend. I just became cool and now I proved it for myself. When we went to the living room, Steve wanted to always sit next to me. Now it was getting embarrassing. I looked at the reaction of his girlfriend and I saw that Steve's action did not send a good signal. After the party, I vowed to myself that I would not be a play-thing. Then one evening at home in Kileleshwa at our family home in Nairobi, the gate-bell rang. I opened the kitchen door and since it was dark, I loudly asked who was at the gate. It was Steve. I asked him to go away. He refused and told me that he wanted to speak to me. I told him to go to his wife. He firmly told me: "I want us to talk". So something in me just commanded me to obey. So I went to the gate and opened. He told me that he'd come to take me out and when I asked him about his girlfriend this is what he said to me: "She just stays in my house refusing to leave. I have asked her to leave so many times. Even my mother came all the way from *ukambani* and asked her to go to her people and that we will get her when we deem it necessary." Steve practically pleaded with me. Anyway I went out with him that evening. We went out to "Bubbles". We had a very nice evening, I met so many of my former college mates and a whole group of people I had been to school with. It was really nice hanging out. I kept introducing him to my friends and I really enjoyed it. Actually Steve was a journalist by profession and at that particular time, he was working as a Public Relations Officer in a top Nairobi firm. Then at the end, he spoke slowly and shyly as though he needed to asked me for a favor. He asked if we could spend the night together. This time I was 25 years old, a virgin and someone who has never been this close in a relationship with a man. Of course I told him no! and he took me back home. I told him to give it time. I told him that as long as that woman was in his house, there were no prospects. I was however becoming a more regular church-goer. I was attending fellowships more often and really shaping up my spiritual life. Then 2 weeks down the road, I heard another gate-bell. This was a Saturday evening. I was kind of expecting it would be Steve, and sure enough he was the one. He hugged me and met me with these words: "She is gone!! She's no longer in my house!" And exited I was! I went jumping into his car and off we went to his house. You can imagine what happened after we got to his home. He took away my virginity that I had fiercely guarded for 25 years. Sure enough his girlfriend was no longer there. And this was Saturday night. By the time I woke up at midday the following day, I noticed he was not in the house. I went to fix myself some breakfast and there was no food in the kitchen. Then I just stayed there miserable. I just slept. I did not want to go home, I did not know where Eric was! I was going nutts!! It was at this time that the spirit of

God was speaking to me and told me that I had taken the wrong direction. I had not however given up on Steve. I prayed that he would be changed to be a God-fearing husband. Then in the evening at about 6.00pm, he came home. I was so happy to see him. He was coming for a change of clothes. He was to go and join his friends for a party. I asked him if I could join him and he said "This is a men-only party......not for you. Stay home and sleep and be careful, if my girlfriend finds you here she might beat you up". I went back home immediately he left. I said this was surely the end of a real spiritual battle. When I went home, I was on my knees and I told God, never again would I hang out with people who are not born-again, never-again would I ever sip wine or any other form of socialization alcohol and I deeply repented for giving my purity to a useless drunkard.

Ladies, I bring to your attention that in every relationship, there is always a lesson to be learnt. I learnt of the wiles of promiscuous men. This man practically lured me to immorality. He was deceptive and moved like a serpent. And he had a personality that easily hoodwinked me. He was soft spoken and very polite. So I knew for sure that he must be a nice guy. Women, beware of men who are promising you marriage and trying to bed you in that pretext. Avoid all manner of unsaved friends who promise you fun in drinking parties. On March 12th 1993 while at a friend's office at the Continental building in Nairobi, Kenya I felt a force kind of pressing on me that if I rejected salvation, I would be destroyed. I was also not getting along with my mother. My parents are middle-class and they were wondering why I could not take a simple job that was full time, instead of being contracted and well paid but going on for some months without work. I was really stressed out. I was under pressure from all sides and I had absolutely no peace in my life!! To actually explain what I felt in the spirit: I had no energy to move on; I felt better dead - but I could not dare take my own life because I knew hell would be waiting for me on the other side; I had the strong feeling like never before, the feeling that I wanted to depend upon the Lord. So while at my friend's office on this day, I gave my life to the Lord.

The following weekend, I went to Kenya High School to see my sisters who were boarders then and I gave them my testimony. I cooked for them a lot of good food and asked them to give their lives to the Lord. The following week when my mother visited them from Nyeri, they gave her the good news: That was a double-blessing and she told them herself that she'd just gotten saved a few days ago.

Exited, they also informed her that I was born-again saying "Winnie also got saved last week!" There was something God was doing in for our family. God commanded my mother and I to get saved on the same calendar month of March 1993. Without any of us being aware of it, God was drawing us to himself. All the arguments I had with my mother came to an end. We now fellowshipped like sisters in the Lord. I however still maintained that I had to leave Kenya because the job market was very depressed and well paid jobs were ridden with institutional politics and sexual immorality and I never intended to be part of that. The most determinant reason for leaving the Kenyan job market was that if a superior at the work-place needed a sexual service from you, you just had to give in - just in order to keep your job. That alone, I could not stand. I was fired from more jobs than I could ever care to count. I knew in my heart that I would only give my body to the man who marries me. I was determine never to use my sexuality as a commercial commodity. I worked in offices where to date, they have lost a whole chain of employees due to the AIDS epidemic. It was like that in Kenya, and also in Botswana. People died in hundreds of thousands. That incident with Steve where I lost my purity just before I opened my heart to salvation marks a very determinant part of my walk with God. I vowed never to have a man touch my body and I thank God that the next man who touched my body was my own husband on my wedding night 14 years later!! PRAISE JESUS!!!

ii) **Please give a deaf ear to society when it pressurizes you.**

Whatever age you are, know that if you are faithful to God, he will bless you with a God-fearing husband and the number of children you desire. Keep this whole worry out of your mind. Of course on the contrary, if you are not sincere in your walk with God, you do have something to worry about. I wedded at the age of 38yrs. By the time I wedded, I had heard enough hurting words from society. DO NOT listen to them. They even tell you: you are getting too old, at least get a baby. Those people telling you such things are a mouthpiece of the enemy. It is one thing for a woman who is not born-again to fall into sexual sin and conceive. It is quite another when a single woman advanced in age tries to advice you that getting a child out of wedlock is good for a single woman. And here on earth, they want you to live a life of a single mother, a life you all know is not the way God intended. Do not yield to that manner of counsel.

iii) **How to socialize with married women:**

When I was growing up especially as a teen-
ager, many people used to say that married women
do not like the company of single women because
they would steal their husbands. But out of experience, I assure you that if you are a morally upright
single Christian woman, married women will be
your best friends. I have a situation of a lady and
I'll call her Veronica. She lived close to me for 5
years at Rockridge in Oakland, California. A different lady Marie who used to fellowship with me
had a complaint about Veronica. Marie confided in
me that Veronica had approached Marie's, husband
and requested that he teach her how to drive. Both
of these ladies are from Ethiopia. Of course here in
California driving lessons can be very expensive and
being a foreigner, it is even more expensive. This
annoyed Marie because it is not all husbands who

respect their wives. Marie's husband went on and taught veronica how to drive regardless of his wife's opinion and contrary to her will. Single woman, DO NOT ask married men for favors. If you desire that they do something for you, make a request through the wives. If their wives say no, then let it be. You need to respect the status of a wife in her marriage. And as you know, in any society word spreads as fast as a bushfire. This story of Veronica spread fast and guess what? No married woman wished to see Veronica around their husbands because you do not know what other 'favors' she could have asked for.

When you are in close friendship with married women, they will give you tips on good marriage, how to be nice to your husband, good housekeeping, children etc. Its no wonder I did not get that many surprises when I went into marriage because I kept close to born-again women who were married.

iv) <u>Do not get involved in 'ladies only' parties whose main aim is to slice and demonize men.</u>

Avoid those parties completely because they only abort your prayers. That is why I reiterate that your largest proportion of friends should be successfully married, Christian women. In those parties single women verbalize negative sentiments and say words like: "I'm Off men", "I don't need a man" "I'll just get a child and live single" "all men are dogs" etc; and all other negative things that really abort your prayers. To prove to you that these kinds of groupings are a stronghold of the enemy, they last for years and years. You can even see people who started these groupings in college and even long after college, these people still hang out together and they are mainly secular. But what did the wise single Christian women do? They grouped up with God-fearing successfully married women, and that way they drew that anointing to themselves and some years down the line, they can only say, "I have seen the fruits". This is because as a woman you should always have that agenda at the back of your mind - that one day you want to be successfully married. You don't wait till you are 30yrs then you start running to church singles ministries. You have to start preparing yourself early. Its all about your relationship with God. Serve him in all ways possible, seek him and you will find him. And it is not about how well you dress, or the perfume you wear! GET REAL and serve the Lord with a passion. And when God examines your heart, he will reward you. Then have a prayer warrior who is fighting for you in the spiritual realm. This is a role that was predominantly occupied by my maternal auntie Mrs. Caroline Gateere who is not only of my blood, but a very powerful intercessor. She is a great woman of God and has a strong anointing for marriage. The other one of course needless to say, is my own mother who only revealed to me what her prayer to God concerning me was. And she revealed this to me after I got married. My mother is an evangelist. She evangelizes for a ministry called House of Peace in Nyeri, Kenya. Immediately I got married, she disclosed to me the contents of her prayers towards my marriage. She used to pray that I got married to first of all: a God-fearing man, who has led the pure life of being a OWM and having no offspring from previous relationships. She also beseeched God that I be married at a child-bearing age. And God crowned all this by giving me just that! Mothers, you should learn to serve God so that your prayers as touching on your children may be answered.

v) If a man does not appreciate your qualities in Education or self-upgrading, leave! totally avoid this kind of relationship.

Women who are well educated are mainly intelligent women. And a man who has a recipe for abuse and exploitation knows that he cannot abuse an intelligent woman because she will find her way out of the marriage as she knows her rights. In Kenya where I come from, men who have the history of wife-abuse in their families like to quote the bible as justification for abusing their wives. They especially like to quote Ephesians 5 "Be submissive like the bible says". Avoid these men who read the bible up-side-down. To them, being submissive means having to stop your career, not arguing with their husbands even when the husbands are out to do things that ruin the family. At one time, a man well known to my family had been out of work for a long time and his wife was the bread-winner. But the man still managed to get money from other sources and go to the bars for his evening round of beers. Each time he came home drunk and needed to remind the family that he was head of the home, he would chase his wife out of the house and tell her "You are just a lodger". He would chase her out, while she's even the one paying rent! A society is judged by the way it treats its women and children. Do not marry a man who does not appreciate your professional and educational attributes. Do not marry a man who has an inferiority complex because I assure you, you will live a life of harassment every day of your marriage. If a man cannot respect you, run away very fast before he marries you. The God-given wife is the virtuous woman of Proverbs 31. If you go to this scripture, you will see that the Proverbs 31 woman was so honorable because she used her genius to make money: considers a piece of land and buys it -v16. "She even makes linen garments and sells them - v24", "she does not eat the bread of idleness - v27"; "she makes tapestry for herself v22": Had her husband not given her financial freedom she would not be financially empowered to so beautifully run her household. Just as the bible aspires us to be proverbs 31 wives, we should pray that the Lord leads us to the Proverbs 31 husbands because "v23 Her husband is known in the gates when he sits among the elders of the land". Her children rise up and call her blessed v28, Her husband also, he praises her. So ladies, if you aspire to have a proverbs 31 husband, you must aspire to be the proverbs 31 woman. But have you ever stopped to reflect on the reason behind her husband's attitude towards her? He gave her all this freedom because he trusts her. As women all over the world aspire to meet that OWM, do we stand to be trusted by our husbands? Are we trustworthy? Do we have integrity? V12 "His heart trusts her because she will bring good and not harm to her life".

Let me note here that I thank the Lord for blessing me with a husband who gives me financial freedom. I know of many husbands who would not even support their wives in writing a book such as this. My husband is with me all the way and even helping me with some of the input. Praise be to God!

vi) <u>Internet dating and Long distance relationships:</u>

Pray as much as possible for the Lord not to lead you to long distance relationships, and do not make a decision on marriage based on a long distance relationship. To many, internet relationships sound exiting and trendy but no!!

Ladies, avoid secular internet relationships. Internet relationships are known to have the highest level of casual physical commitment. The world will tell you "sex is a must as a criteria to evaluate a marriage partner". I will here and now tell you that this is dead wrong. And others may say "oh! but majority of the young people are doing it". And I would remind them that Majority of people are going to hell and in fact, Hell will be full of good people:

Matthew 7: 13 - 14 "Enter ye by the strait gate: for wide is the gate, and broad is the way that leadeth to destruction, and many there be which go in thereat. Because strait is the gate, and narrow is the way which leadeth unto life, and few there be that find it." In this case the word "strait" simply means "narrow".

Your chances of meeting a OWM on secular internet relationships is are extremely low, almost non-existent. I will give you the example of an American lady I will call Bridgette who lives in Sacramento, California. I met Bridgette in October 2006 at San Francisco International Airport when I went to meet Richard and his mom who were away in Kenya for 2 weeks. They had gone to Kenya to meet my family and formally ask for my hand in marriage. In the Kikuyu tradition, a man has to be accompanied by his parent/s to ask for a girl's hand in marriage. They were welcomed with the *"Uthoni"* - traditional Kikuyu wedding (**Also see Chapter 1: e. 9)**. In short, my parents consented to our relationship and Richard and his mum came back to America knowing that Richard was an accepted member of our family and that we could now start arranging our wedding. I was unable to attend this function because my green-card had not yet come through. It was in process and I had to be in the States in case I was needed for any processing interviews.

So it was while I was at the San Francisco International Airport awaiting their arrival at International arrivals unit that I took a sit at the waiting-room café. A beautiful brunette about 6 feet tall joined me as we looked out for the arrival of KLM flight from Amsterdam. As we kept looking out for the arrival of the flight, we struck a conversation and I learnt that she lived in Sacramento, CA. So I asked if she was waiting for a family member and she mentioned that she was so nervous! She was however highly exited as well. She had a bit of tears and her mascara ran a little bit. Her hair was all made! her make-up right and looked ready! She informed me that she met this man on the internet and that they have been communicating for about

6 months. The man lived in Amsterdam but was originally from the Caribbean Islands, though I do not recall exactly which one. Bridgette informed me that why she was so exited was because this was going to be the first time that she would meet this man. She had met him on the Internet and they had a very good rapport. She asked me who I was coming to meet, and I informed her that I was waiting for my fiancé and his mom to arrive from Kenya, where they had gone to ask for my hand in marriage. She said Wow!! I informed her that we were working towards wedding the following summer. She really wanted to know more about Kenya, the people, the food and the culture. So we sat and really hit it well. She wanted to know about our foods especially being a chef herself. So I gave her a description of all the Kenyan foods: *pilau, mukimo, mahamri, githeri, chapati, ndengu* etc, it all exited her. The

137

arrivals board soon indicated the touch down of the flight from Amsterdam. So we left the café and drew closer to the arrival dock. A screen showed the passengers as they came closer to the arrival dock.

Within about 10 minutes, it was her internet boyfriend who appeared first on the screen. Bridgette had blushed all red!! She told me "That's he!" She faced me "Do I look ok?" and I told her that she looked just fine. When he finally appeared they hugged each other and both of them really looked happy to finally meet. She introduced me to her internet-boyfriend as her airport-friend. Bridgette and I exchanged phone numbers, they left and a little while later mum and Richard arrived. They were exited to be back and all Richard said again and again was: "I have to go back to Kenya soon!!!". And sure enough we decided to make it a point of visiting Kenya as often as possible.

As for Bridgette, we continued speaking on the phone. By the time her internet-boyfriend went back to Amsterdam, we spoke a lot. My conversation revolved around my wedding plans. For the first time, I mentioned that I'm a born-again Christian. I enlightened her about the Christian lifestyle especially concerning courtship and dating. It was going towards the beginning of 2007 and she started disclosing to me details of her relationship with her internet-boyfriend: things were terrible!. I told her that Christian dating and courtship excludes sex. She told me "Oh! please, I have to know what I'm buying!". A few months down the line, she knew what she was buying, the man had dumped her and I was headed to my wedding in August 2007. She was hurting, she did not communicate much. I finally, but softly asked her to try Jesus. Ever since I got married, I never heard from her again. It really hurt me to see her hurting like that. For her and for many other hurting women, I prayed that they use the right channels to get that OWM. This is why I am writing this book. If only women knew to do it the Lord's way!

vii) **My experience with both Secular and Christian dating sites**:

In the year 2000, I tried internet dating which was mainly secular during those days. I was in Botswana then, working as a French teacher at a private school in Gaborone, Botswana's national capital. I only went as far as corresponding by email. I mainly corresponded with men from Europe and America. I got the most outrageous emails. They wrote me such sexually motivated emails that I cannot even begin to describe. And of course I decided that this was not the place for me. Long distance internet dating can be very perilous. There have been lots of reported cases of physical abuse and assault by men who have married women as a result of internet dating. It is now the rule in most of the western countries that men seeking wives on the internet from overseas will undergo a thorough background check before Embassies can issue visas to fiancées.

When I came over to the states, a cousin of mine in the East Coast informed me of how a lady in her church met a good husband through a Christian dating site. This was in early 2004. So in April the same year, my cousin gave me the site and I was all set. I paid the subscription that was $25.00 every 6 months. The site opened a page for me and before I knew it, I was receiving emails from Christian men. My web-page had my entire profile which included details like my photo, age etc. To my amazement, even those secular men also started contacting my page. I tell you the devil is a real thief, he goes to where he is not invited. I even got email scum predators who try to con you out of money just because they can see that you are in America. It was so outrageous. By July, there were no emails from genuine Christian men. How I would know that they were faking Christianity is because I would ask questions like: which church do you go to? and he would give the name. What church activities do you enjoy? and he would say, Sunday church services, bible studies, over-night prayers and weekly prayers. And I would say - wow! may I speak to your pastor? and that did it!! That was the last I would hear of the man. They would stop communicating with me from that moment on. What I came to conclude is that just as there are worldly men looking for Christian wives in churches, there are also worldly men who have infiltrated Christian dating sites in search of unsuspecting Christian ladies. That is why we have to be in prayer at all times. Just when I was about to give up in August 2004, I got an email from a member of the US army, a national guard based in Iraq. He was fighting in the Iraq war. I will simply give his name as Ken. He was originally from Texas. I will not disclose his base so that I do not expose his identity. He was active in the military Christian union and worked closely with the military chaplain. He was born-again and he had a very good testimony. He was in his early 40s and he told me that it was his prayer to meet a Godly woman who would make a good wife. I said in my spirit "Yes Jesus! Yes Jesus, this is the man!!! I started going on my knees! I informed my mother about him. Then like never before, we were praying for him around the clock. I informed all my prayer partners, and all those who were close to me in the Christian walk. By September, Iraq had become such a deadly place and both sides were being killed like flies. Whenever he emailed me, I would give him a scripture or words of an encouraging song.

Then a time came and the fighting became so serious. I asked my mother to get into fasting. My mother is an evangelist of the Gospel. She preaches the word to the public. Her ministry is called "House of Peace". Her group preaches in the villages, market places and on the road-sides. You should see how God repays them. They are so blessed! If they pray for you, blessings pour like the rain.

So I committed my mother to pray for Ken. This particular week in October, I had just gotten an email from Ken and he was practically mourning, broken hearted. His very close friend had just been killed in Combat. Just next to him.

Then I asked my mother to increase the prayer team. This very week, Ken went out to combat and the tanker that was ferrying them to the combat ground was bombed. He was incidentally on the exterior. All were killed except him. When their tanker was bombed, even their 1st in command was killed. He wrote me an email and asked me to pray harder. We prayed very hard with my prayer partners and my mother's prayer team.

By October, things were a little bit cooler. He was not reporting as many casualties as before. We eased on prayer. But at that time, there were still heavy casualties being reported by the US military. I never ceased to pray, asking God protect him if he was to be my future husband. Nothing ever indicated that we would not end up together. Then came November. There was heavy fighting in Mosul. I left Oakland for a different part of California where

I spent Thanksgiving each year with the family of my best friend. By mid-day on Thanksgiving day 2004, my heart sunk. I was checking my email and Ken was asking me to pray for him because he was going to leave for Mosul the following week. Those of us who know about the Iraq war will recall that Mosul was a bloodbath city, military planes were being shot down and American militia suffered heavy casualties on a daily basis. I constantly encouraged him with:

Psalms 91 especially v7: "A thousand shall fall at thy side, and ten thousand at thy right hand; but it shall not come nigh thee."

But we kept praying. By December, I had not heard from him yet. But I could feel in my spirit that he was alive and Hebrews 11:1 kept me going

"Now faith is the substance of things hoped for evidence of things not seen". Like never before, this scripture became alive in me. I knew that Ken was alive. At the end of January 2005, I received holy spirit baptism. I was water immersed at the Calvary Christian Center Church in Alameda, California. It was towards the end of 2005 that I received baptism of the holy spirit and consequent speaking in new tongues. I was tremendously exited!

Ken was not communicating all this time, but by the Beginning of February, I received an email from him. I was so exited! He's alive! He's alive! my heart was racing. Then I read the e-mail. He informed me that he was now back to his Base here in the US, having successfully concluded his deployment to Iraq. He did not suffer any injuries and that he was glad to be home. He however said something that turned my stomach inside-out!: he said: "I'm now going back to the internet to look for a wife". If I were in the flesh, I would have written him a very nasty email. But I knew better as a Christian. This man was a spiritual conniver. He exploited the spiritual talent that God had endowed upon me as a way of protecting himself from death at war! When I spoke to my mother, she soothed me saying it was ok and that God was about to give me my own. She even told me that my husband was not very far from appearing. She asked me to be patient.

How I assessed Ken is that if every man were to use a Christian relationship in that manner, this world would be a very good place. It is more constructive than trying to sleep with a Christian woman: Men! take advantage of the spiritual endowment that God has given the born-again spirit filled women!!! Your life will be better.

On the other hand, I have one testimony of a woman who met a genuinely good Christian man on the same Christian dating site. This is what I would say to women who are searching: If you have to go to the internet to look for a husband, please at least try the Christian dating sites and even then, be careful. Have a set of questions well prepared on topics like general living, prayer, bible content - yeah! ask him content questions on the bible. And if you want to be very, very sure of his walk with Christ, ask to meet his Pastor!! If he accepts, well and good. If he does not, hey! its time to move on!

CHAPTER 3

1. <u>Remember your duty and loyalty to God as a Christian</u>

Deuteronomy 6: Talks about how we are to keep God's law in the land we are crossing over to possess. Dispel popular sayings like "Going to Rome and becoming a roman":

Deuteronomy 6: 1 - 7 & v12

"Now these are the commandments, the statutes, and the judgements, which the Lord your God commanded to teach you, that ye might do them

in the land whither ye go to possess it: That thou mightest fear the Lord thy God, to keep all his statutes and his commandments, which I command thee, thou and thy son, and thy son's son, all the days of thy life; and that thy days may be prolonged. Hear therefore, O Israel, and observe to do it; that it may be well with thee, and that ye may increase mightily, as the Lord God of thy fathers hath promised thee, in thy land that floweth with milk and honey. Hear O Israel: The Lord our God is Lord: And thou shalt love the Lord thy God with all thine heart, and with all thy soul and with all thy might. And these words, which I command thee this day, shall be in thine heart: And thou shalt teach them diligently unto thy children, and shalt talk of them when thou sittest in thine house, and when thou walkest by the way, and when thou liest down, and when

thou risest up......v 12: Then beware lest thou forget the Lord, which brought thee forth out of the land of Egypt, from the house of bondage".

So what do we tell the person who recommends that when we "Go to Rome and do what Romans do??" Why don't we re-write this saying and say "Go to Rome and keep your Jesus". When I take the example of myself, I have lived in 4 countries including my own birth country. Could you imagine what sort of human being I would be if I adapted to the Gods of each culture I found myself in? God is telling us not to pollute ourselves with the spirituality of alien lands, because what prevails in the final analysis is the Christian spirituality. When I was a student in France, I worshipped at the American Church in Paris. When I was in Kenya, I worshipped at JIAM ministries, when I was in Botswana I worshipped at a Church called "Deliverance-Baptist, Praise and Worship ". While here in the states in my first 6 years, I worshipped at Love Fellowship Church of God in Christ. After being married to a Praise and worship assistant I now accompany him each time he is to provide services in the various ministries in the Bay Area. The Lord is reminding us that over and above being in different cultures, the culture that should prevail is the Christian culture. And when time came for me to be married, I did not say that I had to be married to a man from my birth culture, neither from this and nor from that culture. I said the man who will marry me will be a Christian. It does not matter whether he was Eskimo, or Aborigine: as long as he was right with God, a born-again Christian, that was my yardstick. God knew my heart and though Satan sent his candidates to me, the will of God finally prevailed.

Let's see what God has to say about his image while mingling with peoples of various cultures:

Deuteronomy 6 V 14 - 19;"Ye shall not go after other gods, of the gods of the people which are round about you (For the Lord thy God is a jealous God among you) lest the anger of the Lord thy God be kindled against thee and destroy thee from off the face of the earth. you shall not tempt the Lord your God, as ye tempted him in Massah..." In reference to Massah, this is where (in Exodus 17) the children of Israel contended against Moses demanding that they should never have left Egypt because they were lacking water in the wilderness and were in a desperate state of thirst.

Knowing that I was determined to be married to a God-fearing OWM, I was fervent in prayer. But time was running out and sometimes I broke down. In 2005, my sister Njoki, younger than me by 8 years got married. Each time I watched the wedding video I used to break down and cry. Especially when I watched the traditional bridal exit that is usually accompanied by women jubilant in song and dance: it is a very emotional moment when the bride is being handed over to her new family and her future mom-in-law takes her and the multitudes of women sing in unison and pray. I used to ask God, What happened to me? I used to sob so loudly that my room-mate would knock at my door and then before I allowed her in, I would cover my head with my blankets and pretend to be asleep.

Then I would finally cry myself to sleep and ask God: "Where is my husband God? eh?.." I would anoint that empty side of the bed and remind God "...Eh? where is he?". That is something I did for a long time. I would say that by the age of 26, I felt ready for marriage. And it was at that time that I kept asking God this question each time I went to bed. I even used to have two pillows: one for me and one for my 'husband'. This was exactly 12 years before I finally got married. God took a nice 12 years to answer my prayer. That very Christmas of December 2005, my sister Njoki called me to wish me a happy Christmas. And she encouraged me and told me: "Winnie, you too will get married, be sure of that" and I answered and told her "yeah! in the year 4000!". That was wrong of me and I repented immediately! We should never confess negative things like those. In a few weeks, I met the man who was to be my husband!

2. **Let them laugh ! *!?!*?:**

At the work place, both men and women always want to know if you are dating or what your love life is like. Men want to know your status in order to know if you are available. And women want to know in order to determine whether to associate with you in matters of the heart. I always make my spiritual status known wherever I work. I openly confess that I'm a born-again Christian. Sometimes they even want to ask you: "You mean you have never..? *!*" and I kept that information to myself. But of course since many work-places are secular, you will usually be the laughing stock. It was very nice to work with Christian married women. They always became my best friends. That is how I came to learn about married life. I would take refuge in their company. It was always beneficial to me. And now that I am a married woman, it not any easier. Men both single and married are questioning why you cannot go and hang out with them for a beer after work. When I show them my ring, they show me theirs too, as though to send the signal "its OK". Extra-marital affairs are so rampant here in the states!. It is even worse when you are a married woman because this sends a signal: if you are married, it means that you are nice enough to be someone's wife. So they try to chase you. Contrary to working in Kenya, America is a much better place to work because if you turn down a date offer, you still get to keep your job. But in Kenya, more often than not, if you turn down a date from an employer or a senior employee at the work-place, you just lose your job. That's the one biggest reason that made me leave my country. In America, sexual harassment at the workplace is illegal. So men are aware of this and they can only go so far. America is the land of human rights and especially women rights, and we attribute this to the fact that in the USA the legal system is vastly founded on Christian principles.

Whenever I went to hospital (during my single days) even though it would just be for a physical check-up, the doctor examining me would ask me what contraception I was using. And I would say "none". And many times I was told "You will get pregnant!!" And I would respond "I am not sexually active". And the most common question I would get was: "Are you frigid?". THE WORLD DOES NOT UNDERSTAND!!. Oh yeah!, let them laugh!

3. <u>Even Christian relationships are do crumble</u>

Christian relationships that are not grounded on the word of God do not have a future. March 2000 found me in Botswana where I lived. I worked as a French teacher at a private school in Gaborone. At this particular time I lived in a part of Gaborone called Block 5, just walking distance form the Grand Palm, Previously known as "the Sheraton".

One evening after work, I realized that I did not need to cook dinner. I had already bought myself a Russian roll from 'Pie City' at the Main Mall, and this pie being so rich left me not needing any other food for the evening. I took a walk to visit a neighbor. Along the way, as I walked past an open gate about 5 homes away from my own, I watched a woman cruise into her drive-way. I really do not know what caused me to stare, but I found myself staring at her car. I did not realize that my staring was so strong that her muscular German-Shepherd dog came out of her front-yard, onto the road and pounced on me, throwing me to the ground and his teeth tearing into my left thigh and my right arm. The days that followed were very miserable but by God's grace, this lady whose dog had bitten me was a senior registered nurse at Gaborone's Princess Marina Hospital. She took full responsibility for my recovery. By God's provision, she was a born-again Christian, a strong woman of faith. Incidentally her dog had bitten a number of people previously and she was advised to take him for re-training at the canine unit. God will always watch over us. Why I am saying this is because this dog had full vaccination and so my treatment did away with anti-rabies shots etc. I got very close to this lady, I will call her Sophie. She came home and changed the dressing daily. Sometimes she took me to hospital, got me a lot of medicine which included antibiotics and vitamins to enhance rapid healing. She gave me her testimony once and I felt that there was a reason why God was putting me close to her. Then one evening, she invited me to her church for Bible-study. The church is a big one in Gaborone's Broad-hurst area. The name of the church is Bible-Life. Actually all through my stay in Gaborone, I never saw a church with as large a congregation as Bible-Life.

It later became a routine: After Sophie dressed my wound, we would go to church for evening prayers and fellowship. Then one evening I accompanied Sophie and her husband to church. As we were exiting, I noticed a man and I could estimate his age as late 30s. He fixed his glance on me and followed me straight out of church. I was not that sure that he wanted to speak to me. But he finally walked straight up to me and asked me for my name. It was dark and we were approaching the church's parking lot. Sophie saw the man approach me so she gave us some time together. Since the man did not have a note book, he wrote my name and phone number at the back page of his bible. He also asked me what happened to my arm when he saw those bandages tied around my right arm. I gave him a brief account of my accident with the dog and he humorously asked me if "I was playing with the doggie". He had a very delightful sense of humor. Anyway he called me the following day. At one time came to pick me at the school where I taught and took me out shopping. In his car, he only played Christian music. He was from Malawi, 37 years of age and a pharmacist by profession. He had never been married but had a son back home in Malawi. I will call this man Kevin though it is not his real name. We had a good friendship going. As my wound was healing well, Sophie referred me to Marina Out-patient and that's where I received daily wound dressing. Then, one time I realized that Kevin was not calling at all. This was about a three weeks from the time I had met him. When I finally called him, he said that he would pass by my place and take me to hospital for my wound dressing. It was a Saturday. I waited for the whole morning, afternoon and evening. Finally I gave up and had to catch a combie (public transport) to go to hospital. I never heard from him for about a week. When he finally came by, it was one late evening, he wanted to come in but I was about to go to sleep. I just allowed him in, gave him dinner. He did not bother explaining about the day I waited in vain for him to take me to hospital, and I did not ask. I was trying to avoid confrontation. Then his cell-phone rung. He stepped out in great urgency. I wonder why he did not want me to hear the conversation. After his conversation, he came back to the house. He told me that he would wish to have a born-again wife of my caliber. I told him to give it time. He then went to his pocket and showed me some condoms. I asked him to leave. He pleaded that he was sorry for showing me the condoms. I told him that it was over. He never gave up. After about 2 months, he came by without even calling. This time, I told him that he could not enter my place. So we just stayed in his car and spoke. I asked him where his Christian music had gone to because when I looked into his Glove-compartment, all I could see was Kwa-ça kwa-ça music. The guy's Christian image was all distorted. This is the kind of man who keeps women in on-and-off relationships, be careful. In church you will meet men who just want to trap the genuine Christian women and deceive them to believing that they themselves are true Christians. Be watchful and keep to God's dating instructions. When this kind of thing happens to you and you are a Christian woman, always fall back to the word for consolation: We know it could be very hurting. Be sure to link up with a victorious Christian, a man of God who lives a bible life. Quit dating defeated

Christian men. And after a heartbreak like this one, just move on and ask God for his grace.

Also let me send this signal: If you are on an on-and-off relationship with a man, be sure that this man is not a OWM. A God fearing OWM is consistent and keeps to his word. He handles matters of time and activity with a lot of transparency. A OWM holds no secrets from his woman.

You can ease your pain of a broken relationship with the words of:

Psalms 46: V 1 - 4

"God is our refuge, and strength, a very present help in trouble. Therefore will not we fear, though the earth be removed, and though the mountains be carried into the midst of the sea; Though the waters thereof roar and be troubled, though the mountains shake with the swelling thereof. Selah.

There is a river, the streams whereof shall make glad the city of God, the holy place of the tabernacles of the most high."

Just pick up your broken pieces and move on, still trusting God for that OWM. Every relationship teaches us a lesson!!

Colleagues at work and people I knew in Gaborone kept pressurizing me to sue Sophie. But I decided to handle it biblically. **Matthew 5 v 25: "Agree with thine adversary quickly, whiles thou are in the way with him; lest at any time the adversary deliver thee to the judge, and the judge deliver thee to the officer, and thou be cast into prison. Verily I say unto thee, Thou shalt by no means come out thence, till thou hast paid the uttermost farthing".** ("Uttermost farthing" .....is like to say - till you have paid the last penny)

Sophie was aware that she had done wrong and she made peace with me very swiftly. She was evidently a very good Christian woman because she handled this crisis Biblically. As Christians we should stop getting into the habit of suing people out of greed of money. Let us run our lives biblically. At work, I was entitled to paid sick-off, Sophie was overseeing my treatment, so what was the need of being greedy trying to pocket some extra thousands of Pula (Botswana Currency). She did accept that she'd done wrong and promptly took the dog for re-training.

4. **Title: OWM in relation to the countries in which I have lived namely: France, Kenya, USA & Botswana.**

France: In the late 1980s while part of my student life found me in France. It is after many years that I realized the reason as to why God did not allow me to settle in France. God had a purpose of using me to proclaim his power to single women who are seeking holy matrimony. Had I lived in France and was married to Etienne, my Christian faith would have ended there**(refer to Chapter 2: f (i).** This would have been responding to a hurried engagement. Etienne wished to marry me within a period of 4 months of meeting me. He was not born-again and in fact he detested the bible and all that it stood for. The life I led in France was very flowerly, but I never had peace, because those days I was not even a born-again Christian, I was just a church-goer. I lived on L'avenue Vaugirard close to 'La tour Montparnasse'. To college at Institut Catholique de Paris, I just needed to walk across rue de Rennes, and then walk two blocks to my left and that found me in college. Classes were great and I enjoyed studies of the French Press system. At that time, Frenchmen found it very trendy to marry African ladies and with the rising immigration crises, this seemed an easy way out for many of these women who were experiencing immigration crisis. Getting work permits was extremely difficult for foreign nationals. In spite of all this, I decided that if I married, it would be for the right reasons rather than out of pressure of any sort. After all, I had a nation, a flag and a home in Kenya. I could honestly not know what else really pulled me away from France. But I was being shown that France was not the country I would live in. It was much later, after getting saved and now being married and settled in America, that God gave me the full revelation. And the revelation was that I was to counsel single Christian ladies seeking holy matrimony, that they should always reject hurried engagements and consequent hurried marriages. There is a reason why God wants us to give decisions on matrimony ample time. Reason being that this is the time God communicates with us and either tells us to move ahead with the marriage or stop the walk into matrimony. Whenever we act in a hurry, we may not be in a spiritual position to listen to the voice of God. To me God had meant France to be a place for me to study, experience my youthful days and have a student-job - PERIOD!

There is a lot that I learnt from France. The French language forms the largest part of my career. Whenever I land a job in an international firm, it is always because I am fluent in French. I have also taught the French language internationally.

Let us now look at the policy of the French government in light of the word of God. It was much later that I realized that it was because of the French secular policy *"laïque"* that God was not able to prosper me in France. America has great religious freedoms and anyone with talent in Christian teachings is more likely to prosper here in America than in France. I still have not given up on France, it is a great nation with a very rich culture, but I can also come on board and put in word that will help prosper the country in even further. "France, expand your religious freedoms and God will bless you and multiply your riches. Furthermore, encourage spirit filled Chrisitian missionaries into your land and you will see increased prosperity. When you do good to others, it always pays off. These Christians pray over your country and they leave multiple blessings". The Lord wanted me to be in America so that after experiencing these liberties and being a success story of the American foreign policy, I would bless young Christian women all over the world with my life story. Had I accepted hurried matrimony to Etienne in France **(Chapter 2 f-i),** my life story would have ended there. There would have been nothing for me to share with single Christian women in the world. Also, when a Nation blesses individuals, and those individuals happen to be Christians, be sure that they will pray for God to prosper the nation that has hosted them.

We can see this in a book that I would urge you to read. It is entitled "A voice in the midst of A storm" by Evangelist Suzzane Njuguna. This book just goes a long way to prove that the destiny of a nation can be determined by the spiritual standing of those living in it. In Suzzane's book, you will read of how God-fearing people who have been welcomed to the USA have come to call America Home. See for yourself how these God-fearing immigrants pray for the Nation and the results that follow.

Recall in the Book of Daniel when the 3 Jewish boys were in Babylon. See how the Babylonian Rulers valued them, and see how God used them to turn around the future of Babylon. We may think that this just happened in bible days but I assure you that it is happening today, here and now!

When you study the book of Daniel, you will see that even though Nebuchadnezzar (Daniel 2) had taken Jews captive, he lacked the spiritual strength to control his kingdom. He sought spiritual support from the very people he had captured, and this is because they served the true and mighty God. He had to listen to their spiritual counsel for his own survival and because of the holiness of Daniel, Nebuchadnezzar (Daniel 3 & 4) was turned to a God-Fearing man. Towards the winding down of the book of Daniel, we are shown how the Kingdoms of the earth will have to bow down to God. The book of Daniel closes on a note of the end-times.: "The abomination that causes desolation": Which means that more than ever before, we should prepare ourselves for the end of the church age and the rapture of the church of Christ.

Kenya:

Kenya is my birth-country and has a great history as a nation. It is known as the gate-way to East Africa. Those of us who have been to Kenya know that she is a very unique country in that her tourism in unmatched in the world over. Like all other countries, Kenya too has her weaknesses. On the social scene, statistics have shown that it is very common for worldly men to go to church in search of wives. They deceive the unsuspecting women. And women who do not keep to the word of God find themselves trapped. Yes these men marry them but alas! their true colors emerge once they are in the marriage. The men go back to their former lifestyle, partying with their mistresses and painting the night clubs. You will be the laughing stock of his other women and who will indeed take time to taunt you usually when they are partying the night away in night clubs in the company of other high-flying girl-friends of married men especially when they are on an all-women-*'heng'* (party) reckoning: "...... lady of the house, - you keep the ring, while I keep the man!!!!". And they usually celebrate with long episodes of unison laughter... So you can imagine who the loser in this scenario is! YOU! the poor married woman at home! You are trapped at home with children and a non-resident husband. This is because the legal system in Kenya has been extremely deficient. Women are left to fight for the survival of their children, frequently having to take the law into their own hands.

The oppressed woman in Kenya

If you are dating a man who does not encourage your personal advancement and does not appreciate your high level of education, begin leaving him as soon as possible! In Africa where I was born, the largest proportion of men do not want to marry educated women. When they marry you and you have a career, once you get married, they can even manipulate you to discontinue working. And then after that they dictate to you the number of children you should give birth to. So finally you are jobless and penniless and then you have a line of children. It will leave you with no choice but to fully depend on him because he is the only source of financial power. You will practically be a slave to him.

You will find that your life will be so complicated because you will be expected to sing a song whose words and tune are unknown to you. It is usually hard for the African woman. And of course this is a recipe for manipulation and the man can easily have as many extra-marital affairs as he wishes because you are safely locked up in the house. And divorce being the most difficult procedure especially in an African Country like Kenya, none of you will break off easily. Then worse for the woman, you are stuck for life. In Kenya, a divorce ruling can take very many years to come through. So the nature of this law causes the marriage to remain "bona fide". This in a way is an advantage for the children who will have a home to live in though the parents are not in harmony. But it causes men to have an oppressive grip on women: they abuse you and there is nothing the society can do about it and the worst of it is that

HIV - Aids and other sexually transmitted diseases are slowly but surely waiting for you! In Kenya, my birth country, the only safe woman is the one who knows God in truth and in Spirit. The Lord will deliver her through and through!

Coming back to my parents, I vividly recall an incident that took place when I was about four years old. I was asleep and I shared the bedroom with my brother Johnson who is one and a half years older than I. As I slept, I heard loud cheers and it must have been very late in the night. The cheers were accompanied by laughter and a lot of jumping. These noises woke us up and we left our bedroom going towards the living room. My parents were jumping up so high, holding each other and it was like they were both trying to score a basket on a basket-ball pitch. In fact they were jumping like *Masai Morans*. They did not even hear us come in. They just kept

on jumping and laughing loudly, cheering and in tre-
mendous joy. My mother's face especially was full
of tears of happiness. When they cooled down, they
tried to explain to us that my mother had just passed
her *Pitman's* short/hand(Stenography) exam with
100.w.p.m. Being four years old at that time, I did not
quite understand about school but I could vaguely
recall my mother drilling her shorthand into the late
night hours for a long time. But I didn't realize that
it was such a big deal. In short, this is the college
certification that landed my mother employment as
a senior secretary in the civil service since the beginning of the 1970s. She's now retired. It was much
later on that they explained to us that my father who
had a higher education than my mother, helped her
to acquire training that would make her employable
in the job market. He assisted her by paying her fees
and giving her all the moral and material support

she needed. Kenyan men, I'm talking to you: when your wives need to upgrade themselves even when it means going to University, PLEASE, PLEASE, assist them. If you have a Bachelor's degree and she wishes to get a Master's degree - please support her. In edifying your wife, you edify your own home. And when you do good to your wife, you are actually doing good to yourself. Even when you do not have a degree and your wife needs to get one, please support her! I have my paternal uncle William who lives in Nyandarua district, in Central Kenya. He does not have a University degree, but had a long standing career as senior primary school teacher. He is currently retired. When his wife who was also a primary school teacher decided pursue a University education, he supported her all the way. This is what even the word of God calls a real man! Let us hear what the scriptures have to say about husbands and wives:

Ephesians 5: 25 - 27: "Husbands, love your wives, even as Christ also loved the church, and gave himself for it; that he might cleanse it with the washing of water by the word, that he might present it to himself a glorious church, not having spot or wrinkle, or any such thing; but that it should be holy and without blemish."

<u>CRUCIAL</u>: V 28: "So men ought to love their wives as their own bodies. He that loveth his wife loveth himself, for no man ever hateth his own flesh but nourisheth and cherisheth it even as the Lord the church"

USA:

The American law is very swift to protect women and children who become victims of dysfunctional marriages and relationships. In fact contrary to the laws in countries with conservative legal systems, the American legal system causes the irresponsible party to financially, physically and emotionally support the offspring of an estranged parental relationship. I overheard some Kenyan women here in Oakland once mention *"Huku Americani wanaume wadanganyifu hufunzwa adabu njema"*. (America is where deceptive men are taught good manners!)The legal system in America teaches parents to take full responsibility of the consequences of sexual acts. Even though it were a fling, as long as it has brought fourth offspring, you will foot the responsibility of raising that child till he/she is eighteen years of age. It is known as the child support system where the government causes the parent to pay child support through his/her employment, and as we all know, there is no escaping and whoever tries to escape is just digging a hole to fill another.

Botswana: In the late 1990s, I worked in Gaborone the capital city of Botswana. This is the most peaceful country I have ever lived in. Due to it's well run economy, the population is well catered for. Botswana is a major exporter of Diamonds and Beef products. Another factor favoring Botswana is that its population is very low. So resources circulate easily and crime is almost non-existent. However, when I lived and worked in there, the rate of HIV infection was 60%. The "death industry" is a booming business in Botswana. By the time I left Botswana in 2001 to move on to the USA: Morgues, funeral homes, caskets and all that appertains to death and burial was a rapidly growing industry.

At that time, there was a government commercial saying that combating AIDS is as easy as ABC. A-'Abstain'; B-'be faithful' and C- 'condomize'. This is because the Batswana society is so promiscuous to a point that Aids is an accepted part of life. It was reported that the average Batswana will decline to have a HIV screening test. And all this is because Men are not faithful to their wives, and then the single women get deceived into sexual relationships with these married men with an aim of convincing them to abandon their wives. And before they know it, they have been sexually involved with a string of men and vice-versa. What I learnt however is that the Batswana women who are faithful to God always came out clean. There are those who were on fire for the Lord. They remained faithful even in their single lives, patiently waiting for that God-fearing man to propose to them. But the vast majority of married women are glad to co-exist with their husbands' mistresses/girlfriends. They have taken sexual promiscuity as the norm. This is rather disturbing because it may look right to them and of course this is tantamount to welcoming the sure coffin that awaits them at the end of the road. This is why the rate of HIV infection is so high, the bereavement business is booming, and AIDS orphans are uncountable. We as Christians have to pray for the world. I do however have a lot to thank God for. In as much as there is a high-scale promiscuity, there is a powerful Christian population in Botswana. The Church in Botswana is very strong, and we know that the will of God will ultimately prevail.

<u>Conclusion</u>

a) Women, if you are to receive anything from God, be prepared to obey his word, meditate upon his ordinances, pray fervently and fast consistently: **2nd Timothy 2: v 5: "And if a man also strive for masteries, yet is he not crowned, except he strive lawfully...."** Many other translations give the same message ie. in order to win, we have to play by the rules.

b) And sure enough, there is a reward at the end. The largest proportion of OWM have been seasoned by the word of God and hence adhere to moral and spiritual discipline. Be sure that the Lord is a rewarder of those diligently seeking him - **Psalms 25 v 3: "yea, let none that wait on thee be ashamed: let them be ashamed which transgress without cause."**

c) And when God gives you that OWM, he is the man who deeply loves you, and whom you deeply love. I do remember the words of **Philipians 4:8** that my maternal uncle Minju Kariuki shared with us on our wedding day as he traveled to the States from Kenya in the company of his wife Beatrice (when she married into our family on Dec 2nd 1979, we used to call her 'auntie Princess' because of her beauty. Time has proved that she's not only beautiful on the outside, but also very beautiful on the inside. We love her very much!)

A group of close relatives also traveled along with them to the States from Kenya just to attend our wedding. This is the scripture Uncle Minju shared with us:

Philipians 4:8 " Finally brethren, whatsoever things are true, whatsoever things are honest, whatsoever things are just, whatsoever things are pure, whatsoever things are lovely, whatsoever things are of good report; if there be any virtue, and if there be any praise, think on these things."

When you occupy your mind with these words, there will be respect, joy and prosperity in your marriage. When it is all crowned by having God at the center of the marriage, there is nothing the two of you cannot achieve!!

CPSIA information can be obtained at www.ICGtesting.com
Printed in the USA
BVOW082119190513

321049BV00001B/2/P